Pyramids of Light

To Jan —

Pyramids of Light

It is all Possible!

Awakening to Multi-Dimensional Realities

Blessings

Meg Blackburn Losey, Msc.D., Ph.D.

First Printing 2004

ISBN 0-9753223-0-3

Cover design: © 2004 by Meg Blackburn Losey
Author Photograph: Maria Gurule
Editing: Marti Senterfit and David Losey
Interior Graphics: © 2004 by Meg Blackburn Losey

Printed in the United States of America

Dedication

To the One... of which we all are...

Our perfection is Divine...

Table of Contents

Table of Figures

Acknowledgments

So many people touch us in our daily journeys through life and there are a few without whom my life may have made different turns.

To the "core group" who graciously and generously welcomed me into your forum, encouraging me to become comfortable with my gifts even when those gifts went beyond bizarre! In the group's beginnings: Joan, Cathy, Lynn, Harriet, John, David, Laura, and Paula, and later: Van, Pat, Betty, Jean, Billy, Sue, Gina, Andrew, Nora, Bill and Doris and all who came and went in between. It is many of your questions that are answered in this book. You became my spiritual family. Each of you is a beautiful light that will be with me always.

To Christie with whose encouragement and support I stepped out of hiding and began to share what I had learned... you built it and they came... thank you.

To all the thousands of light workers on my "list" who have supported my work by your input, your prayers, and your interest. Thank you for your loving encouragement.

To Jane at Winsome Design, who humorously and diligently assisted me in the creation of this book cover, thank you.

To Marti Senterfit, my editor and assistant - two halves really *do* make a whole. Without your assistance and attention to the little details this book would still be an unpolished manuscript. There will never be enough words or enough ways to say "thank you". I am ever grateful for the day that you literally walked into my life saying "what can I do?"

To my husband David, your love and support in everything that I achieve are the very essence of what love is...thank you for being there through the hard times as well as the good ones. I appreciate you more than words can say.

And to the Masters who came when I was desperate to know the Truth beyond our everyday illusions, who patiently taught me day after day about life, about living and about the Light within all things, and have remained to guide me, I remain humbly of service.

Foreword

By the Masters as a group message to the Reader
(As channeled through the Author)

(Note: No other part of this book is Channeled. The author feels that since it has been the Masters who have tirelessly and lovingly brought forward information, it would be appropriate to have them introduce this book.)

Greetings, Dear Ones. We are grateful to be of assistance to you at this time. In your quest for Truth it is that you seek in many directions that which you wish to learn. It is that as you look outwardly that you are denying your most valuable assets… yourselves. You see, it is that of which you are created which is the very thing of which all things are made. That which is Light. It is also the source of your power, your strength of being.

In such a way, that Light which is you carries the memories of its infinite journey which ultimately manifested as you. As this is so, the memories of those journeys long past are resident within you — all of them, from beginnings in timelessness to this now when time seems so important to you. Time is yet another limitation that you instill upon yourselves.

It is only to look within for that which you seek in Truth. It is all there. It is to utilize that which is Light for your journeys in each moment, to be present with yourselves and looking to no other for answers, for each of you holds a different set of Truths.

Each of you is comprised of frequencies of Light, each of you with a unique signature of frequencies of different vibrational combinations, different sets of harmonics that carry the memories of all time within you and the memories of the journeys you have chosen in your paths and passages.

In such a way, the truths that you seek begin with that which you need in order to raise the essence of Light within you. To each of you, those truths may look just slightly different. After all, you are experiencing from your own unique set of energies!

It is to remember that you are a part of all things, all things being you. In such a way, lack of perfection is only a perception. And any and all perceptions can be altered with a simple change of your minds.

Once you have given yourselves that which you need in this way, you will begin to know the Truths that you have so long forgotten. We have brought forward for you teachings that will assist each of you in your journey from within — first with explanations as to the how's and why's and, later, practical application to your individual experiences.

Use that which feels appropriate to your personal journey. It remains to be your choice in all that you are and do. What you accept and what you do not becomes of the choices you make along the way. The tools that are given here are that of a place where there is no time. That which is in and of the essence of being. That which is the One. That which is Light.

There is no restriction upon what you may become as a being except that which you perceive as imperfection of self. That, Dear Ones, is an untruth. You cannot become an untruth, only live it. You are perfection in every way in every moment, and, this said, it is to remind you that you are a living, integral part of a much greater whole, a contributive aspect to All That Is.

The information that we have brought forward to you from that which is Light is to remind you of that Light from which you came, and how it is that you may utilize this Light in a conscious way toward remembering the perfection that you are. Further, to remember how to create reality beyond anything that your thinking mind can imagine. To create that which you intend, leaving that which you do not desire out of the process.

In such a way, you are the creator of your reality, of your destiny, of your journey, no matter which direction it may take in any given moment. You have the power and the strength to create change of direction not only within yourselves, but in the world in which you live.

As you read, we will assist you in your perceptions. If you are uncertain of that which has been given, listen with your heart, rather than your mind, as there are Truths which do not fit the rational self, only that of the heart — which is the pathway to unconditionality of spirit. It is there that your answers lie.

Be in peace.

And so it is that we return to Light...

Shalom, Na'hallah, Namaste.

Introduction

I began my passage into other-dimensional realities after experiencing a severe dark night of the soul. Upon evaluation of my life up to that time, I did not like what I saw, and decided to change my direction completely, shedding the uncomfortable "safe zone" that I struggled to live within and giving myself fully to make those changes.

As I moved through my awakening, I began to have experiences both consciously and energetically beyond anything that I had ever encountered. As new experiences occurred, I asked, and even begged, for more understanding of what was happening to me.

One morning after such pleading, the first Master appeared in front of me. He manifested as a hologram, and began to lead me through exercises that later became my passageway into higher knowledge, rites of healing and fantastic journeys into the unexpected and unknown. The unfamiliar felt quite familiar and I knew that life as I had previously experienced it was history. After the first lessons were given, other Masters came in a procession which led to multi-level learning and, later, intentional multi-dimensional existence.

What I began to realize was that for the first many years of my life, I was living narrowly within lies that others had given to me as Truth. The goals I had set for myself were not mine, and my accomplishments meant little to the me who had been buried by the rules and ideals of others. In all of that, I found freedom of self.

During my discovery process, I had a multitude of questions which over time were answered first by the Masters in fragments, then as entire lessons which seemed to absorb into my very being as knowings of greater truth. I remember wanting to know it all in a day. Everything! But what I realized was that if I had been granted my wish, my cosmic equilibrium would have been knocked so far out of whack that I would have lost all touch with reality in this world. There is much to learn, and it is an infinite process.

I wanted to share some of what I have learned. Perhaps using this information will change your lives in some positive way, as mine continues to change. Letting go was the key. Forfeiting all sense of controlling my life and allowing myself to tumble gently through great waves of knowledge and into what I sense to be an inner wisdom. Time will tell.

This book contains the basic principles of life and enlightenment as shared with me by the Masters, as I lovingly call them. It is a compilation of numerous years of communication and journeys with Masters from extraordinarily high dimensional planes. Where possible, facts and theories relating to the subject matter are backed up scientifically; however, there are many issues which are addressed that are far beyond the measurability of modern science. Quantum physics and string theory only begin to scratch the surface of the universal construct as well as our relationship to the All. This is not a "how to" book, rather a book of possibilities that the reader may explore for him or her self.

As we begin to understand our part within the whole of creation, we then begin to understand what Truth and reality are from a wholly new perspective. As we do so, our very perception of all aspects of existence changes.

Our values transform, and we begin to operate moment to moment from a very different platform of being. Our awareness of our environment, ourselves and others increases dramatically, and synchronicity becomes evident on a large scale. We develop into more intuitive people, learning to let go of our perceived control because we know — really know — that control is an emotional, ego-based ideal. It has no place or effect in reality except perhaps to divert us from the path we intended. We learn how to become *of the One*, rather than working *at* it.

Stepping out of perceived reality, the social mores that we are given by our predecessors and those who have purported authority over us takes a lot of courage. We are given boxes of realities to abide by and those boxes become our safe zones because those beliefs are all we know. Rarely do we step out of those safe zones unless we are pushed by great changes in our lives.

We bump along, feeling that there is something larger looming just outside our comprehension, but have no idea how to access what we sense. Many of us at one time or another — or still — believe that some form of religion holds the answers. Yet often there are more questions than answers, and when we are given an answer, it has been translated out of truth or context, which changes the meaning of our answers from what was intended by the original ancient scribe to someone else's intentions. At best, religion is a format, a context, in which we can feel the spirit within us.

We are given God as a strong-armed thunderbolt of a character with a temper, and told to pray to Him for forgiveness. In this context, we are powerless and become beggars for what we want or need. Somewhere along our historical path we have lost sight of the God within each of us. As a whole, we have become vulnerable wimps who have given our power to anyone who displays confidence or certainty, even when that leads us into avenues we do feel to be Truth, and therefore many of us turn to spirituality. Ahhh, even the name has a good feeling! And a great connotation: spirit-u-ality. I am spirit. You are spirit. Now we are on to something!

But it all seems so nebulous. When we study metaphysics we are often told of "the light", that we need to "manifest", meditate toward higher consciousness, the I AM, miracles, being "in the moment", travel beyond our current place and time and many other terms that end up being ideas that we can't quite connect with. Yet we know in our hearts that they are very real. So what does it all mean?

In this book I have written a step by step approach to answering those questions by taking the reader on a journey from the beginning of consciousness through all aspects of manifested creation and into facets of conscious being. I have also included exercises which were designed by the Masters and me which lead to greater comprehension in easy steps. What the reader will find is that it is all so simple, all of it. Life, creation and our relationship within it...no mathematic formulas necessary, no long term experiments — it simply *is*.

True ascension is not necessarily leaving the body, or even taking the body to other heights of reality. It is a process of enlightenment. It is about coming full circle back to ourselves as integral parts of a living universe. It is about our quest for home and — during that quest — honoring the spirit in one's self and all others.

As we become enlightened, we become of Light. Those parts of us which have manifested since the Beginning start to awaken and harmonize as frequencies of Light. Our vibrational rates become higher and faster as our literal being-ness becomes more and more of the very Light from which we are created. Once we begin to understand this process, we can function as ascending beings, walking within the third dimension and translating higher knowledge throughout our human experiences, both in our own experiences and those of others.

Many people, particularly in current times, are having other-dimensional experiences that cannot be explained when compared to the old ways of thinking. Many hear voices, or feel energy through all or part of their bodies. Others are becoming more intuitive or having visions of people, things and events that do not fit their current perception of reality.

Countless people who begin these awakenings become afraid of their experiences, and ask everyone they know or worse, no one, what is happening to them. As a result, what was the beginning of a beautiful gift becomes shut down out of fear rather than being utilized toward a greater experience.

The point is that *there is nothing to fear*. There are indeed other realities of existence which often overlap into each other, even into the reality which we thought we knew. Finding the courage to step out of our old belief systems which have functioned as boxes that were neatly created for us by others, is only a matter of changing our minds toward accepting greater reality, fuller experience and not attempting to quantify or measure those experiences in any way. Attempting to define our experience generally results in misperception or a logical ordering of that which is illogical within our current forms of understanding. Either, when taken into our thinking minds, may become fearful simply because it is out of our frame of reference.

Stepping into other realities also requires a complete lack of expectation. For when we expect our journeys to look or feel a certain way we are generally disappointed, or become stuck in those expectations, thus limiting our experience. When we allow ourselves to *become of our experiences* rather than *becoming* our experiences, we begin to exist from our sacred selves and our sacred selves have always known the way home.

Historically, we have convoluted what we know inherently by our perceived needs to survive and communicate and by our perceptions that each of us is a separate entity in a vastly faceted manifestation of creation. In fact, we are consciousness which has saturated every particle of a physical body for knowledge. What experiences we choose and how we interact within those experiences to gain that knowledge is up to us.

Change is a good thing, even when we don't think so at the time. Open yourselves to changes in awareness, explore All That

Is for your own answers. Use discretion when you get those answers; ask your heart, not your head or anyone else, how those answers feel deep within you. Remember to breathe, and remain open to new realities. It is my wish for you, dear readers, that as you move through this information, you will find a glimmer of recognition within yourselves as aspects of a far greater thing that becomes a bright beacon, lighting your way home. That Light is already within you...

Namaste

Section One

We ARE

the

One

Chapter One
In the Beginning: A Genesis

In the Beginning there was Darkness. The Darkness was a living, writhing entity, its density seeming unforgivable to all but the inkling of Light deep within.

The Darkness expanded outwardly from its center, moving slowly, writhing from its depths, and as it did, the Darkness developed a predictable rhythm. Within that rhythm a regular, pulsing movement developed. Each time the Darkness pulsed, each time the Darkness moved from within, it used energy, and as the energy was expended, there was a frictional response within the Darkness which resulted in the formation of more energy. The energy which was formed was Light. The Light began to grow, filling all of the space in the heart of Darkness. As the Light grew in volume, it pushed the Darkness farther and farther outward from its center of beginning.

To understand this process better, we can compare the creation and use of energy to what happens when we create electricity for our use. Much of the electrical energy that we use in our everyday life is created in a similar way. Electricity is created by generating frictional reactions of one kind or another from the power of water, heat, or even nuclear materials. When those reactions take place, energy, or — power as we call it — is created.

Whatever the source, energy pulses in regular frequencies, just as the universe does. Power that we generate is harnessed and sent to us in a variety of ways. That power exists of different intensities or frequencies. When electricity escapes from where it is harnessed, such as from wires or generators, it sparks or arcs. Both the sparks and arcing are visible as flashes of Light of varying color and intensities. If we happen to be touching the source of the power as it escapes, we can feel the pulse of that energy in the form of an electrical shock. The universal energy system is much like this. The universal energies are more in the form of electromagnetic energy, which is of a higher vibrational frequency, or pulse, than electricity as we know it, but the principals of creation and expression are similar. We can feel that energy, and it can be utilized and directed for a multitude of uses (see Figure 1).

Figure 1: The Energy Cycle

The production and consumption of energy in the form of light is an infinite cycle from the Source outward into the Universal process and back again. During the sequence from creation to consumption, from one frequency to the next, the light retains all memory of what it has experienced. As it returns to the Source, the light brings with it all that it has recorded, adding the information to the Universal consciousness.

Another example of how Light energy works is what we see when static electricity is present. For instance, when we walk on a carpet, we collect energy. That energy builds up in our bodies as it is collected. When we touch something after we are charged with the static electricity, there is a spark as the energy is released. We can see this spark and feel the energy as it is released. Sometimes we can even see the energy spark as it is released. By virtue of our own movement we have contributed to the creation, collection and expending of energy.

And so it is that out of the Darkness came that which is Light – energy in its purest form.

As the Darkness continued to move, pulsing and writhing from within, more energy was created, the volume of Light grew, and the Universe began to expand. As expansion progressed, the Darkness was pushed farther and farther outward. There came a point in the expansion that the mass of the Light outsized the Darkness. In All That Is, there became less and less room for the balance of power between the Light and the Darkness.

As the mass of Light grew, not only did it push the Darkness in an outward manner, the Light illuminated the center of the Darkness, and the Darkness, being more dense, naturally sought balance with the Light. Ultimately, the abundance of Light became too great for balance to occur and a shift of cosmic proportions occurred. The Darkness collapsed upon the Light.

In the instant that the Darkness fell upon the Light, the Light was smashed, fragmented into incalculable splinters flung outward in a spiral motion throughout all of What Was. The Light was dispersed throughout all of creation and, as the Light traveled, the Darkness became further illuminated. From the process of collapse came an expansion of reality. The Darkness was no longer Lord of creation.

While the Light sped outward, it gathered memories, a consciousness, of all that it had been from the Beginning and all that it experienced within its journey. As it moved upon its path, the Light chronicled virtually everything that it experienced. Each particle of Light was experiencing an individual journey, so each tiny fragment of Light retained a series of memories individual unto itself.

All of those memories were in energetic form — that form being pure Light energy arrayed as a group of frequencies which *was* the memory. As the memories were held within the Light, each tiny particle of Light developed an individual frequency or set of frequencies based upon its experience. Each particle of Light became a harmonic signature unto itself.

Because of the retained memories of its individual journeys, each fragment of Light existed with a reality that was slightly different than any other fragment, even though the experiences were similar. Each distinctive set of frequencies and tones became the identifying factor of each fragment of Light, and within that uniqueness, an individual consciousness as well.

As the fragments of Light began to slow from their initial propulsion, the process of natural ordering began. All of the fragments of Light were attracted toward other particles which had similar frequencies. Although none were exactly the same, the Light fragments began to gather with other particles of Light which had comparable experiences.

Because of the unique frequencies that had developed within each Light fragment, as the particles of Light began to order, the new formations of Light began to harmonize within their individual aspects and Universal balance began to unfold.

The principle of natural ordering required the Light to order with the least difficult process. In doing so, the particles of Light began to align in order of both shape and harmonic frequency.

These alignments ultimately became holograms in the form of four sided pyramids.

(A hologram is a field of Light which reflects a scene or an object so that it appears three dimensional, while maintaining both the amplitude and phase of the Light in that field. The scene has no solidity, but is recognizable in every detail.)

Each side and base of every holographic pyramid contained individual sets of frequencies. Thus, each pyramid that was formed became an individual entity with a harmonic combination that became its signature identifier, unique from all other pyramids.

The holographic pyramids contained the memories, the consciousness, of the Source (the original Light from which they had come), and the collective experiences of each of the particles that had come together in the creation of that pyramid. *Each pyramid maintained an individual reality, a living consciousness.*

Each pyramid also retained within it the spiral motion which was reminiscent of the moment it was propelled from the Source. This spiral motion, rotating clockwise, contained a full spectrum of color and frequencies of energy.

The frequencies of the spiral were aligned from the bottom of the pyramid up. The longest, or base, frequency, which demonstrated as the color red, resided at the pyramid's widest place, or base. From the base as the spiral moved upward, it followed a full spectrum of color. Each level of the spiral gradually shortened and moved through all of the color frequencies, which included energy and sound frequencies. At the apex of the spiral as well as the pyramid was the same pure frequency of light that had originated at the source.

Holographically, each pyramid contained a sphere. The sphere was the center of all creation, the memories of the

25

Beginning, the eternal reminder of the One from which the formation originated. As the spheres formed within the pyramids, they began to rotate in counter-clockwise motion (see Figure 2).

Figure 2: Polarities within the Pyramid

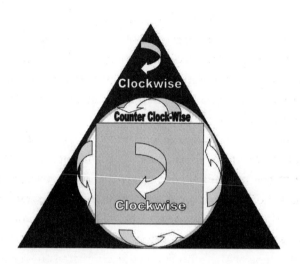

The sphere contained collective memories of the Source. Those memories were in the form of perfect Light. The sphere maintained balance within the pyramid in the same way that a gyroscope balances the direction of a rocket ship. The sphere became an internal portal for each pyramid to remain connected to the power of the Light, the internal heart of Being which continually changed its conscious perceptions of reality as each pyramid interrelated with other pyramids throughout the ordering process. A collective consciousness was beginning to become reality within the tiniest aspects of creation.

Every one of the pyramids also contained a cube which nested within the sphere which had already formed within the heart of the pyramid. The energy contained within the cubes began to rotate in a clockwise motion in an opposition of polarity to the counter-clockwise flow of the sphere within the pyramid. The combination of the clockwise energy in the spiral, the counter clockwise energy in the sphere and the clockwise energy in the cube in that final formation brought perfect balance within the interior of the pyramid.

Natural ordering continued and the holographic pyramids began to seek other pyramids that were familiar in structure and memory. As they began to collect, the pyramids began to arrange themselves one among the other. Eight at a time, each apex pointing to the center, bases outward, the pyramids structured themselves into holographic octahedrons.

Each octahedron carried one unique set of harmonic frequencies, or realities. Every one of the octahedrons inherently carried all of the unique sets of frequencies which comprised each of the eight holographic pyramids and each fragment of Light from which the pyramids were created. Each octahedron retained consciousness of the Beginning and all of the collective experiences from which that octahedron was produced. These octahedrons became the particulates, or building blocks, from which all things are created. They are the fabric of the Universe.

As with the fragments of Light and the holographic pyramids, the octahedrons began to seek out other octahedrons which were familiar. As they came together, the octahedrons began to organize in an alignment according to harmonic relationships within the bases of the eight pyramids which formed each octahedron. During this alignment, differences of polarities within the octahedrons logically created space between the holographic octahedrons from one to the next. Empty hallways of space formed between all of the particulates. These spaces, or null zones, became the balancing factor among the particulates. They

also became communication highways throughout the universal structure.

As above, so below – the holographic octahedrons ordered next to, above and below each other. From the first particulates to the dimensional realms, no matter the size or form of creation, all planes of reality were shaped in this same fashion and pattern. From the tiniest model of the particulates came a repetitive pattern of octahedron formation. Reality had begun to manifest in various forms of expression.

Dimensions were produced both inwardly and outwardly in the same format, comprised of the same octahedron shape. Each dimension had its own set of frequencies, its own reality, based upon its position and alignment within the entirety and the frequencies of its makeup. The farther outward from the origin of ordering the dimension occurred, the higher its frequencies became. Moving outward from the Source, or the center of creation, the higher dimensions carried frequencies that were closer and closer to pure light.

Figure 3: Octahedron Patterning of Particulates

As above so below, manifested reality took form as octahedrons which aligned by their flat sides, leaving null zones in between.

The sum of all things looked much like a giant honeycomb (see Figure 3). Historically, from ancient temples in Egypt such as the Temple of Osiris and other initiation temples as well as through time immemorial, the infinite process of creation has often been depicted as the Flower of Life (see Figure 4).

Figure 4: The Flower of Life

Flower of Life represents the alignment of particulates within the universal construct. This is an infinitely repeating format.

The *Unified Field Theory* describes reality as being of a uniform construction which has both a strong and weak force of energy. While it has not to date been scientifically proven, this theory is quite correct in its assumptions. Universally, the strong force of energy is comprised of the particulates. Each holographic octahedron, or particulate, was created of an individual set of harmonic frequencies. Those frequencies were energy. The strength of these combined energies lie in both the uniqueness of the complementary combinations of those frequencies and the collective whole of the fragments and pyramids that comprise that particulate — plus the collective memory, or consciousness, of each aspect, all of which is continuously changing because the experience of that particulate is constantly varying!

The weak force of energies as described in the *Unified Field Theory* was comprised of the empty spaces, or null zones — those hallways of space between the organization of the octahedrons. The empty spaces serve a two-fold purpose. First, the empty zones create a balance within the Universal structure, a series of equal spaces which act as a cushion within the construct which allocate equal space between the particulates. This spacing creates an equal balance throughout the construct of creation. That balance is maintained as energy flows through the null zones. This is what keeps the particulates from falling on top of each other, which would result in a chaotic mass of unorganized energies.

Secondly, the weaker energies which comprised these null zones originated from the emissions of frequencies and ever-changing polarities of the particulates. These emissions filled the empty spaces of the null zones. As the spaces inflated with those emanations, a universal communications corridor was formed throughout the fabric of creation.

When any individual, group or series of particulates had an experience, that experience changed the interior makeup of the particulates involved. The frequencies changed; often the polarities of the charges within the particulates changed as well. The experience was communicated through the null zones as electromagnetic emissions were discharged during the changes within the interior of the particulates. Those communications or electro-magnetic energies moved along the interior of the null zones. As they did, they informed all of the other particulates along the way of the changes that had just occurred. The other particulates, receiving the information, reordered or changed their frequencies accordingly. Thus, with each incident, a new reality began.

As the particulates communicated among themselves, receiving messages from every level of creation through the null zones, they responded to the messages they were receiving. When frequencies were emitted and traveled into the null zones from the particulates, they created new and different harmonic relationships with each particulate that was passed.

Responding to the new and different harmonic relationships, the particulates reordered themselves to align with the new harmonic frequencies. The reordering consisted of new alignments of the flat sides of the octahedrons. As new alignments came about, different realities began to manifest. Matter was created and worlds were born in all dimensions of existence, of reality.

From the Source of all creation Universal evolution began, and as it did, the memories of the entire process were collected within the Light that was the source of all the realities that were created from the Beginning. A constantly growing collective consciousness was born.

Chapter Two
The Manifestation of Matter

The collective particulates continued to order and reorder and, as they did, amazing things began to happen.

The particulates which formed the fabric of reality began to change in response to the communications they received through the null zones. As the energies of those communications flowed across the sides of the particulates, and the particulates responded by reordering, the harmonic resonance which was created by the new alignment became new realities.

Since not all of the harmonic alliances were the same, different realities began to originate. Those particulates in the outer dimensions, the ones with higher vibrational frequencies and memories closest to the Source, began to manifest as a living consciousness. This consciousness had no definable structure and remained formless. It was filled with infinite content and continued to collect memories of the experiences of all the particulates as they ordered into new realities. This consciousness continues to store and communicate information at the highest of levels even now.

From the highest level of existence came an inward manifestation of conscious life. The construct of life was based upon the principles of light. As manifestation continued to move inward, it did so in spiral form. Due to the weight and compression of each preceding layer of reality, or dimension, the particulates and the light they contained became more and more dense as the inward dimensions were formed. Therefore, so did the matter.

Each dimension which was created resulted in a slightly different aspect of consciousness.

Each aspect of consciousness became a reality. That reality began to take form: those beings created of the outer realms, having little to no density, manifested as Beings of Light, infinite creatures living within the consciousness of creation. These beings of Light ultimately became a bridge of communication between the lower realms and the Source.

At different frequency levels, or dimensions, the living consciousness organized and Beings became of different awareness and purpose. Those in higher categories retained much or all of the conscious memories of the Light. They became those who would defend the Light from intrusion by Darkness, sharing the memories of the Light with those of lower vibrational frequencies.

Moving inward through the dimensions, other Beings of Light began to manifest. These beings displayed as a multitude of living color, which contained all of the colors of the spectrum. As these Beings moved, it was as if they were created of liquid light. Color flowed with every motion of their magnificent spirits.

Others of Light were created within the higher realms, each with a different perspective of Being, each having somewhat different aspects of conscious awareness, each level having a purpose in the entirety of all things.

As the manifestation process moved farther inward, there became levels of great mentality. Those born of this great mentality became links between the above and the below. They retained the knowledge of the processes of development, both of the outer realms and the inner realms. This information was stored, for the most part, in scientific format, symbols created of Light which contained complete expressions of information about the characteristics of Being and the process of returning to perfection.

These more cognizant types of Beings, beginning to experience the density of the inner realms, did not have a complete sense or memory of the perfection of the Light from which they came. Instead, their sense of perfection became information oriented and based upon the accuracy of their data. There was little to no emotionality retained in those realms.

Moving further inward in dimensional construction, below the mental planes came the formation of more emotional planes — those where existence was based almost purely upon the sensory aspects of being. The emotional planes ranged from chaos to bliss yet having some remaining sense of mentality. The mentality and the emotional perceptions confused each other greatly and a third aspect developed. This third aspect ultimately became the human ego within the third dimension.

Within the dimension of the third came the development of mass and structure. The densities aligned to form solid manifestations, first of galactic magnitude and later with more refinement — the development of life in corporeal form. Due to the density of construction, life in this realm retained only slight conscious awareness of its origins and contained many emotional and mental aspects which had filtered down from the manifestation of the higher dimensions.

Galaxies formed and within them, checks and balances became a natural occurrence. Everything formed of a spiral nature; Light expresses itself as nebulae, stars and other celestial bodies. During these formations as the Light recreated itself, black holes twisted into existence, draining off excess pressure in the given reality. Planets formed, spiraling masses with an abundance of energy at their centers. As the mass of the budding planets gathered, energy was created within those centers.

The surfaces of the forming planets remained mobile around each center, floating upon heated masses of molten debris that had come together to become the planets. Vents developed upon the surfaces of the lands to release continued discharges of energy from deep within the planets' centers. Gravity was formed due to the spiral motion of the forming planets, and moved at the speed of light. In this way, another balance occurred and the planets retained their positions, as did the stars and other celestial bodies.

Parallel universes began to take shape, feeding off the excesses of those universes around them. Infinite realities spun into existence, each one subsisting on the universes which had formed around it. Consciousness of different levels continued into each new reality.

The consciousness among those who developed below the fifth dimension began to operate outside the consciousness of the Source. Those who manifested in these levels began to consider themselves outside all other aspects of manifestation and creation. Their density did not allow for the remembering of Light and therefore restricted access to the collective consciousness.

Those of the third dimension began to create for themselves illusions of existence which grew into a lesser reality than that of the One Consciousness of the Source. Those Beings began to perceive emptiness within and only *possibilities* of a greater reality, for they had forgotten their perfection. Unfortunately, for the most part, although there was a tugging memory just in the background of their awareness, they couldn't quite remember what it was they had forgotten.

The most inner realms became those where the remnants of Darkness had fallen. Within those realms resided vileness and hatred, secrets and lies, as the darkness had fallen to the densest aspects of being. The density was such that the Light did not penetrate beyond the Darkness and the Darkness raged within all of creation. The Darkness fought to be free of Light, manifesting dark warriors; semblances of being that were of despicable nature. Each time the battle raged, the Light and those who had manifested of the Light were victorious and the Light grew in power and strength. The Darkness seethed in its failure.

Each time the Darkness lashed out more Light was created, as the energy of the Darkness created the same friction that had allowed the Light to outgrow the Darkness in the Beginning. The Light perpetuated and deep within the heart of Darkness was created yet other inklings of light. In this infinite pattern of the formation of all things lies the continual promise of new creation.

Within the Darkness, the Light will continue to expand until once again there comes an immense instant of imbalance between Darkness and the Light and another flash of cosmic rebirth will occur.

Chapter Three
Conscious Being

The Difference between Consciousness and Thought

As human beings we are aware of our consciousness in many ways through the awareness of our thoughts, but *our thoughts are not our consciousness.* Our thoughts are a series of electrical impulses which attempt to create logic in this dense physical world based upon our need as physical beings to survive, to understand, and due to the evolutionary process which occurred during the time we learned to communicate with each other.

In the Beginning, we were all telepathic. We retained some connection to the universal consciousness and had no need for words. We knew instantly what we needed to know, as our consciousness brought to us a constant stream of information from within each universal moment. In human form we began to evolve to denser forms of functioning as survival became a forefront concern. Our brains began to localize our brainwave patterning. In the process, our brains began to use less and less of their functioning as transmitters and receivers of the ever-flowing universal information. Our consciousnesses became buried under evolutionary changes.

Other beings came into our realities and inter-bred with those who had evolved naturally on this planet. As hybrids on this planet began to migrate, interbreed, trade and so on, some form of communication became necessary. We began to use forms of sound that mimicked our environments. The songs and calls of birds, clicking like some insects, grunts and other sounds from animals and nature developed over time into recognizable language that was ultimately spoken.

The mind, the thinking brain, had to work harder in a different sense. It had to listen to words which were different than the melodious harmonic sounds and pieces of information that are carried through the universe during its natural process. Those words had specific definitions that must be understood. Soon nuances played a part in interpretation as well. How the word was spoken and how the body expressed itself during the speaking of those words had everything to do with what was being said. Multiple communication levels began to develop. The mental, thinking self evolved farther and farther from the conscious self. The ego also began to play a part in the way that communication was changing. The ego began to judge, to praise, to confound and confuse communications as they came in as well as when the communications were made. Eventually we evolved away from our pure telepathically communicative skills and into a convoluted mess of interpretive interaction.

Often the consciousness and the mental self are confused as one and the same. The mental self is the one that argues in our head, justifying our experiences and judging our performance (along with its counterpart, the ego). Our consciousness is easily recognized as that part of us that comes in from left field with an idea or information that is completely foreign or seemingly irrelevant to the thoughts we are having in that moment. Many call this their "higher self" but often have a hard time distinguishing thoughts and ideas from pure universal inspiration.

During the human evolutionary process, the thinking part of us overcame our awareness of the natural processes of our consciousness. The memories of everything that we have retained since the Beginning are all there; we have just lost touch with that part of ourselves.

As we began to communicate, we developed a need to think about *what* we were going to say, about *how* what we were about to say might be interpreted, and about what *effect* our words might have once they were released. After all, words are energy too. But we forgot that part somewhere along the way.

The further we progressed in the need to communicate with words, the more we began to think. We began to justify why we would say what we were thinking about. We began to dissect what the people who had spoken to us really meant. We became caught in mental cycling, repeating the same thoughts over and over in our heads until we forgot what the original question was. Our perceptions of the original subject of thought became distilled with all our processing until we barely recognized the truth. This became a behavioral pattern throughout humankind.

For many millennia we worked at perfecting our forms of communication, moving farther and farther from the simplicity of being in touch, tapped into the Universal consciousness, until at some point we began to believe that individually, we *are* the Universe, and that all things revolve and happen around us.

Of course during this transition, our emotions became a part of the mix too. And so every time we have a mental process, it triggers chemical releases throughout our body which stimulate our genetic structure to signal the body to release chemicals. Those chemicals activate our emotions which in turn activate more chemicals which in turn — well, you get the picture — one big thinking, feeling cycle of stagnant existence. No forward motion. Situations perpetuate and repeat because there is nothing obvious telling us to change direction or to stop the cycle. This is what happens when we become stuck, attracting the same type of situation over and over again in our lives.

The most profound results of the evolutionary process relating to our consciousness are twofold: First, there is the idea of single human being-ness as being separate from all other things. That separateness connotes individuality. Much of that individuality in this day and time feels empty and unfulfilled because we are no longer in touch with the universal process — not only that of which we are made, but of which we are an integral part. Secondly, most humans look externally for answers to fill that emptiness, for instructions to a better way of being. Those answers are within each of us, not in books, on the internet, or in the opinions or experiences of other people.

Many people who have found the internal connection attempt to share their methods and experiences with others in various ways. They give step-by-step instructions on how to have an experience just like the one they had. Some people benefit and some do not. What we need to remember is that each person is having an experience individual unto him or her self, that each of us is operating at his or her unique frequency level. So while experiences may look the same or similar, they do not always feel that way because they are not.

Remembering Our Connection Within

The answers that we all seek are within us. Each answer we get is similar to what another seeks, yet not quite the same. The emptiness which people in the world today are trying to fill is a lack of recognition of self. Cultural and internal awareness in the world today has become diluted by virtue of too much input from too many sources over too much time to the point that we barely recognize ourselves as beings of value, of Light. Deep within us something stirs and we know there is more — we just don't know what it is.

We need more than to be still and listen. We need to remember how to use the tools that we have carried within us since the Beginning.

Fortunately, due to many factors at this time, we are evolving full circle into beings of higher consciousness, sharing inklings of remembering — from deep within our awareness — who we are and what we are capable of doing. Once we have begun to understand the simplicity of our true Being-ness, there are no limits to what we can create from within our reality. Or what we can do within that reality.

So now we have a basic concept of how the Universe is put together and we know that our minds are different from our consciousnesses. We know that the answers we seek are within us. Sure, but how does all of this apply in real life?

We are created in the same way that everything has been made since the Beginning. We are fashioned of a group of particulates which has come together as the reality of us. The particulates which manifest as the reality of us are arranged in a logical, harmonic order and communicate amongst themselves from within the null zones.

Each of us is unique because combined; our collective sets of particulates carry a unique harmonic signature which is our personal universal identifier. In other words, we can be identified aside from all other things in creation by the set of frequencies that are us. Harmonically, those frequencies make a sound that is very special. That sound cannot be duplicated on any level of reality because it is created of all of the frequencies which are contained within the very particulates of which we are made.

Remember that those particulates originated as fragments of Light that collected memories all through their journeys. Those fragments then formed into pyramids and ultimately as octahedron-shaped particulates. The combination of those particulates created the uniqueness of us.

Our personal harmonic frequencies hold a very important place in all of creation. In our own way, we contribute to the balance of the universe. Our special harmonic sets are a part of the communication system within the universal construct. There is no other manifestation in any level of reality which has the same set of harmonic frequencies that we have.

Our harmonic signature is our identifying factor universally. Every person, every being, every place — and yes, even every event in time — carries these unique harmonic signatures.

In the entirety of all things there is only one of each of us. We cannot be duplicated, for each of us contributes uniquely to the wholeness of the universal harmonics.

Within our uniqueness is carried an awareness of all the experiences that we have had since the Beginning, just as the light fragments carried all of their memories in Chapter One.

That awareness is created of those energies which are stored within us, in our particulates, as harmonic frequencies, as Light. *That awareness is our consciousness.*

Our consciousness is our essence, that part of us which has traveled throughout our lifetimes, maintaining our harmonic signatures throughout our journeys. Our consciousness lives within each and every part of us.

Our consciousness is energy — pure and simple. It is the same energy that has been an active part of all creation since the Beginning. Our consciousness is that part of us which is *actively participating* within the Universal construct toward creating and retaining our reality.

The memories retained within us are not only *our* consciousness, but a part of the Universal consciousness as well. As our consciousness experiences reality, it is expending energy which moves through the null zones of the Universal construct — first in our local area of reality, or dimension, then both outwardly and inwardly throughout the different layers of reality, communicating our experiences all the way.

We Are Multi-Dimensional Beings

In the same way that our consciousness inter-communicates with the universe, the universe communicates with our consciousness. Energy from the universal communications network that moves through our null zones brings us information on a continual basis. That information changes constantly, and as it does what we are able to perceive as accurate information from "out there" can be recognized when we are in touch with ourselves beyond the illusions of three-dimensional realities.

With our consciousness both sending and receiving information fluidly, we exist on all levels of reality concurrently. While we may not be aware of it on a cognizant level, all of our realities are working together with some awareness of us as whole beings while we experience many realities at the same time.

Our consciousness is aware of other dimensional levels of existence and by that awareness, actually exists as an aspect within those other dimensions. It is in this way that we can experience multi-dimensional realities simultaneously. But more about that later...

Becoming the Moment

Many belief systems stress the importance of "being in the moment". We ask what that means and why we are supposed to let go of everything that is going on in our lives or has already occurred, and just pay attention to one particular moment. The truth is that *everything only happens in a moment*, never in the past and certainly not in the future.

Everything that has ever happened, any time or anywhere, did so in one moment.

When we are living outside of our moments, what we are doing is attempting to control our experience either by reliving the past or by looking ahead of ourselves into the future where everything is only speculation.

If we remain conscious of the moment in which we exist, we intentionally act as an integral part of the One. When we insist on remaining in the past — which is gone — or in the future — which is purely conjecture — we confuse our process of creation by telling it things that are irrelevant. The only *now* that matters is this one. In truth, there is no other time to create. When we send out messages into the null zones that contain our feelings and thoughts of past experiences or fears of future events, we are sending mixed signals into the null zones.

What we are really saying to the creative universe is that we may or may not intend to create a reality but we aren't sure because we were injured by our previous experiences. Or worse, we are afraid of what might happen in the process of attaining that reality. Whew! And so what happens? Usually nothing. Or, we end up in a pass or fail situation where we have limited ourselves to what we hoped or what we feared. And getting to the realization of that new reality is usually a struggle. Obstacles get in the way, things come along unexpectedly, and one delay after another comes along and ultimately we give up or accept less than what we intended in the first place.

Ultimately we become less focused on the reality that we mean to create because *we are not participating in that reality*. Instead, we are becoming stuck in *what was* or *what has not yet become*. As we remain fixed in our focus, we are sending that focus through the null zones, out into the universe over and over again so the universe responds by recreating over and over again the same kind of situations that got us stuck in the first place.

When we position our consciousness in the moment, letting go of past experiences or concerns about future experiences, we become more highly aware of what is happening both within us and around us. We become an intentional integral part of the universal process from *within*.

We become the moment. We act as the One. We become the creator.

As we become the moment, we shed all thinking and emotional processes that delay the reality that we are trying to create. We voluntarily become a part of our own process.

The Light which is within us begins to recognize unfettered paths toward the reality that we have begun to create. We begin to see signs which lead us in directions that we might not have taken if we had not been paying attention in that moment. We begin to experience synchronicities, things that seem perfect in their timing and execution, almost as if planned.

We are often amazed at the perfection of events in a given moment when we have dropped our worries, forgotten to try to understand, and instead participated from our most perfect viewpoints... our consciousness from within the One. When we do so, we add information to the universal process that tells the universe that yes, things are going right and we would like more of the same!

Creating the Reality We Want

Each time we make a choice in our life, we change the path of our consciousness toward the results of that choice. In the moment we make a choice, we affect all that we are and all reality in the Universe simultaneously. As we expend the energy of that choice, that energy is communicating throughout the corridors of the null zones. The particulates along those corridors rearrange, creating a different set of harmonic relationships which therefore creates a new reality.

When we insist upon continually repeating reality by becoming stuck in the process of what *was*, we do not progress because we are holding the energy from within our consciousness, our Light selves, toward the past. That energy condenses and ultimately traps any effort we make toward escaping the past.

When we become focused upon what *might* happen or what *could be* as a result of any given situation, we are creating from our fears. We are creating from a standpoint of less than perfect belief in the reality that we wish to create and therefore sending those doubts and fears into the creative process. What we send out we get back. It is a rule of natural law.

In essence and in fact, we are the creators of our realities. From our consciousness we can, by virtue of choosing it, create any reality for ourselves that we wish simply by creating that reality as a part of our consciousness. As we project a reality that we choose to create into the universal process, *we must believe unequivocally that that reality will manifest.* Since we have projected this reality into the universal aspects of creation, *this reality has already become actuality.* We are then simply in the *process* of attaining that new reality.

The trick to creating reality is to focus on the outcome rather than the process.

It doesn't matter how many times we project the new reality into the Universe. One time is enough — that is, as long as we haven't sent all our doubts and fears into the null zones with this new attempt at creation. When we project our doubts and fears into the quotient, we limit the outcome to only that which we have projected or less. Our intended reality becomes a pass or fail situation. We have limited our outcomes to less than we desired (see Figure 5)!

When we project our new reality into the Universe with the belief that it has *already* occurred, we have given that new reality room to grow into any amount of fullness. Simply stated, we have given ourselves infinite opportunities for limitless possibilities of manifestation of our reality.

When we project passion along with an intended reality, the passion acts as a propulsive energy. It also gives strength to the energies that we are sending out. As a result, the energy of our intent moves not only more quickly, but as a strong, full signal to the universe that we mean what we have asked (see Figure 6).

The information travels with a greater power of speed and clarity, moving faster and farther into the creative process and bringing our new reality to us without delays or confusion as to what we have commanded.

Figure 5: Intent

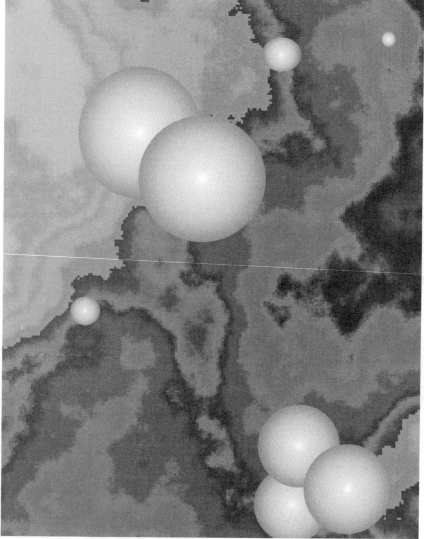

Intent which is put forth into the null zones with doubts or fears moves in a scattered fashion with each segment of the intent communicating a different reality.

Figure 6:   Intent Without Doubts, Fears

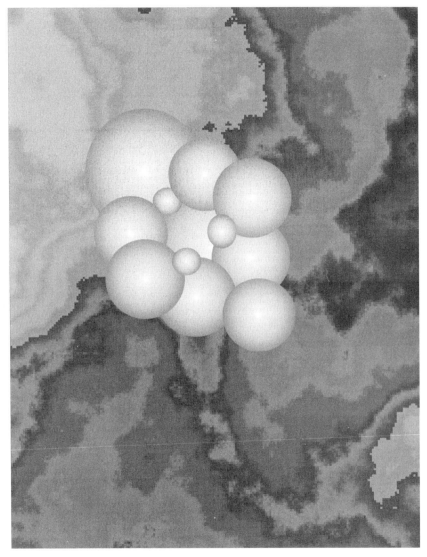

An intent that is sent out into the creative process (particularly with passion) from within the moment moves as a cohesive bundle of information that soon becomes the reality that was intended.

It is in this way that prayers work. We have all heard of cases where people came together and prayed for the healing of another person and that person miraculously became well. Those prayers were projected *with passion* for the healing of that person along with the *belief* that a difference could be made — *total belief* in the power of those prayers.

In those cases, the people who prayed were creating a new reality through their passion. They literally *created* the healing through their prayers. The prayers were conscious energy that was sent out into the universal process with passion and belief that that reality would be so. And so it was.

Perfect results of manifestation come from a purity of intent with a solid belief in the outcome of the intended reality. The power of passion fuels the emission of conscious energy toward the outcome of the intended reality.

The Pyramid Exercises

We now know that we are made of Light — that Light having formed into four-sided pyramids and further into octahedrons, all in holographic form. We know that we are essentially a consciousness which is the same type of energy as everything else. But how, as solid masses of humanness, do we safely make the transition from solid form to consciousness?

A bit of explanation may be helpful. Since the basic form of the Universal construct is the pyramid, we can begin there. The upright four-sided pyramid is representative of our consciousness. It is the true Trinity of being. The base of the pyramid represents us. The apex, or tip, represents Spirit, God, The One or whatever name is a comfortable reference for you. The center of the pyramid is the perfection of the combination of the One and Us. The center is also where the sphere is found.

Geometrically, the circle or sphere represents a never-ending connection, with its exterior enclosing infinite possibilities. It also represents our consciousness and us as beings. Without some sort of guidance in the center of the circle, the interior is energetically chaotic, with all of the possibilities bouncing off the circular walls with no anchoring energy or direction. There is no balance.

When we insert a dot in the middle of the sphere, that sphere becomes balanced. A relationship between the center and the exterior of the sphere is formed (see Figure 7).

The dot in the center of the sphere is the same as the apex of the spiral...as if we are looking at a spiral from above. (This also applies when you are looking at a pyramid from the top down.) The tip of the spiral is representative of the One. The Source.

The peak. The tip of the spiral is the highest frequency in the entire universal construct. It is Light at its highest form.

The tip of the spiral as well as the tip of the pyramid can be imagined as the balancing point of the sphere or the pyramid. It is the most perfect aspect of each of these geometrical shapes. When inserted into the center of the sphere, the tip of the spiral (which looks like a dot in the center of the circle) is representative of the balance we find in ourselves when we allow spirit, or Light, to guide us.

Figure 7:   Circle with Balance

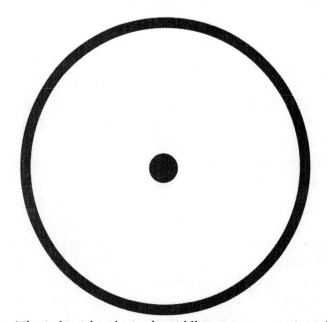

The circle with a dot in the middle represents our universal relationship, with the interior dot balancing all the possibilities represented by the never-ending circle which forms the exterior. This diagram is also representative of the Light within the Darkness with the outer dimensions being of Light and the interior dimensions being denser until the center is reached. The center contains the Light which will ultimately form a shift in current reality.

Similarly, when we think of the pyramid, the tip represents perfection, or spirit. The center of the pyramid becomes the area where we are joined, One with perfection, and the base being our selves as individual essences. When the aspects are combined in this way, the pyramid is a perfect representation of the trinity within us, the One, Us and the combination of the One and us.

A myriad of possibilities continue to exist within the circle but are no longer swirling aimlessly within the sphere, rather existing in balance and harmony. In this same way, when we consciously allow ourselves to reconnect with the One we become balanced.

This is our infinite relationship with the Source described geometrically.

The following exercises assist in the exploration and recognition of the different aspects of our consciousness. These exercises were given to me by a group of Masters during my own journey, and shared in a group experience. These exercises are amazing in that the depth of perception which may occur is profound. The extreme of disembodied sensations during the experience is merely a beginning toward awakening to new realities.

These exercises also allow for us to experience a perception from each aspect of the Trinity of being. First, self as an individual disembodied consciousness, secondly as the Universal Consciousness and thirdly, as a combined One within the Trinity of Being.

As with any exercise of consciousness, please remember that *you are always in control of your experience.* If at any time you find that you are uncomfortable, simply ask to return to the state in which you were prior to beginning the exercise. In other words, to return to your body. It is as simple as that.

Week One - The Upright Pyramid

It is important to enter this series of exercises without expectations or any intent. These exercises are simply for the understanding of your connection as a purer consciousness within the Universal process. During this exercise, you can use the four-sided pyramid to experience yourself outside the denseness of your body. By doing so, you will begin to understand yourself as an essence that is quite separate and different from the body that you presently inhabit.

It is best to do these exercises in the order that they are given both for the quality of the experience and the fullness of your understanding. Skipping ahead does not mean that you will learn this faster — only that you will have lots of pieces of information that don't yet fit together to make sense.

Figure 8: Upright Pyramid

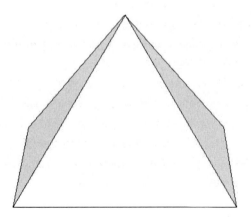

To begin, close your eyes and imagine a pyramid that is created of Light. It has no density. The Light is a golden yellow and the form of the pyramid is comprised of millions of tiny little dots of that Light. (If you can't quite picture a pyramid, start by imagining a triangle.) The pyramid is four-sided and larger than your body. Imagine that this pyramid is floating in front of you and that you can step inside it. This pyramid that you have envisioned is a hologram (see Figure 8).

When you feel comfortable with this image, imagine that you are stepping inside the pyramid. Once you have stepped inside, imagine that you are sitting down inside the pyramid.

Once you are inside the pyramid, one of the first things that you will notice is that you feel free and light. The air you are breathing may begin to feel cold in your nostrils and you may hear or feel a slight but consistent hum. *The tone of the hum that you are hearing is your unique harmonic signature.* The tone, or hum, may seem to have a pulsing from deep within your perception. Your tongue will automatically move to the roof of your mouth.

Experience this feeling. Notice what it feels like to be free of your body. Notice that the energy in your body has become different and that you feel very connected to everything at once, yet you remain aware of yourself. You may have other visual or aural experiences during this exercise.

(It is important to note that you are always in control of your experience. If at any time you begin to feel uncomfortable in any way, simply stop the exercise.)

Experience the feeling within the pyramid as long as you are comfortable and able to maintain the experience. Then simply desire to return to your physical body. Notice how you feel... clearer, lighter, freer. Balanced and more in touch.

Congratulations! You have just taken your first step into multi-dimensional awareness!

If you wish, do this exercise for a week or more until you feel *very comfortable* with the energies and the experience. If it helps, take notes to track your progress. Gaining a large degree of comfort within the pyramid will assist you in the next phases of the exercises.

Week Two - The Inverted Pyramid

Now that you have experienced yourself as pure consciousness in the form of an upright four-sided pyramid, you can progress into the Universal perspective. To do this, close your eyes and picture the same kind of pyramid (or triangle) that you worked with in the previous exercise and, with your imagination, turn it upside down.

Figure 9: Inverted Pyramid

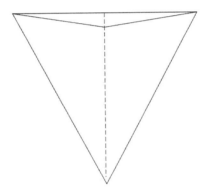

The pyramid now looks much like a "V", or a satellite dish, a receiver of sorts. Once you have obtained this image and it feels comfortable to you, use your consciousness to step into the inverted pyramid (this may be a bit more difficult than the first exercise until you have practiced a bit because the energy within the inverted pyramid is quite different than what you experienced within the first exercise) (see Figure 9).

Having stepped into the inverted pyramid you have intentionally joined the Universal consciousness.

Allow yourself to sit with these new energies. What do you hear? What do you feel? With your ethereal eyes, what do you see? Each of you will have your own experience with this part of the exercise because you are each made of different sets of frequencies. How your awareness perceives this experience is based upon what frequencies you carry within you.

It takes longer for some to understand the information they receive in the inverted pyramid while others who work with this exercise will quickly understand. Since there is no competition "out there" beyond the third dimensional reality, it really doesn't matter how long it takes you to "get it". With practice the information will come and the experience will broaden.

Some of the information you receive while in this inverted pyramid may be in conceptual form, while other information may come to you with fine details. *It is important not to think about what you are receiving — just let yourself receive.* In the moments that you are doing this exercise, you have joined the Universal process in real time. You, in those moments, are intentionally receiving information via the null zones of the universal construct which is communicating to your personal particulates. You are intentionally being a part of the information flow throughout all things. You have become the moment.

Do this exercise, if you wish, for about a week or until you feel that you have mastered consciousness from within the inverted pyramid. Pay close attention to your perceptions during this part of the exercise as they will be quite different than those of Week One.

Week Three - Putting It All Together

Now you have experienced yourself both as pure consciousness and as an intentional member of the consciousness of the One. This exercise will teach you to pull yourself together on Universal terms... with a few surprises...

To do this part of the exercise, you must close your eyes and picture two pyramids one upright, like the pyramid in the first exercise, and an inverted pyramid just like the one you worked with in week two. Once you have created the pyramidal holograms, step inside the inverted pyramid. After you are settled inside the inverted pyramid, imagine that the second (upright) pyramid is being lowered on top the pyramid you are occupying – as if someone is putting the lid on the lower, inverted pyramid (see Figure 10).

Figure 10: Combined Pyramids

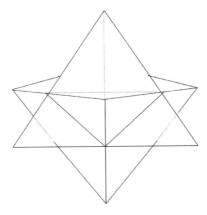

As the upright pyramid is lowered onto you within the inverted pyramid, ask the upright pyramid to turn forty-five degrees so that the corners of the upright and the inverted pyramids form a star on the exterior. Lower the upper pyramid down two thirds of the way over yourself within the inverted pyramid.

You now have a complete representation of yourself as a conscious being within the Universal perspective. You may begin to hear your harmonic signature again. In a different environment, such as another planet or dimension, this tone or combination of tones would sound different to you. This has to do with local environmental harmonic resonance.

The energy that you feel while you occupy this geometric formation is quite powerful. It is as if you are in the middle of all creation. You are. As mentioned earlier, within each pyramid resides a sphere of energy. That energy represents perfection just as it did within the formation of the holographic pyramids that ultimately became the particulates. Of course when you are working with holograms, the spheres within the pyramids become holographic too. They have shape and dimension, and they spin.

As the two pyramids join — one upright, one inverted — the spherical energies within the pyramids are spinning. As they are placed one on top of the other, the spheres — now globes of spinning energy —begin to flatten out. For a short while, from a side view the flattening circles begin to look like an infinity sign (an eight on its side). The energies of the two circles wobble briefly as the two come together and then in an instant they open up together, releasing the perfect energy which has been held within in their centers.

As the release of Light, of perfection, occurs you will experience that Light as a moment of rejoining perfection from within your consciousness. You will become intentionally present in the God energy, the energy of the One, the Source.

Within the star formation that you have created, you have also created, from a conscious standpoint, your Merkaba. Your Merkaba is your energetic transportation anywhere, any time, in any occurrence of any event that has, is or ever will happen. Many people have created the Merkaba using the three-sided pyramids. These will work but they are not as easy to control.

It is important to note that what you think about while you are in this star formation may possibly manifest immediately so it is important to clear your mind of all other things.

There are many who utilize the Merkaba for traveling throughout the Universe, other dimensions and so on. Navigation is simple once one has learned to access the Universal signatures of the people, times or places which they wish to visit. One uses one's own unique set of frequencies both to travel outward as well as to return.

When you are using it, your frequency signature looks very much like sine waves. Sine waves are sound waves that look like a number of letter "S's" lying on their side all connected end to end. When you are traveling within the Merkaba, using your own set of frequencies as controls, as you move away from your body, those "S's" stretch out with less and less curve the farther you travel and the frequencies rise to a higher rate of oscillation. The process is a lot like projecting an elongated spiral toward your destination. When you return, those "S's" regain their curve and the frequencies gradually become lower and slower in oscillation until they have returned to your normal and unique frequency (see Figure 11).

Since both your body and your consciousness carry the same set of frequencies, and you are using these frequencies for navigational purposes, you are not likely to get lost in your travels. When you begin to apply other tools of the Merkaba, it is imperative to have a working knowledge of those tools so that you remain safe in your travels and stay connected to the life that you have chosen in this here and now.

Figure 11: Sine Waves: During InterDimensional Travel

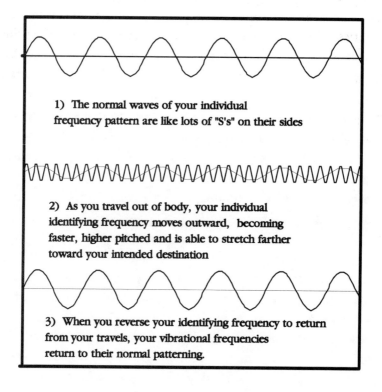

1) The normal waves of your individual frequency pattern are like lots of "S's" on their sides

2) As you travel out of body, your individual identifying frequency moves outward, becoming faster, higher pitched and is able to stretch farther toward your intended destination

3) When you reverse your identifying frequency to return from your travels, your vibrational frequencies return to their normal patterning.

I have found that it is entirely unnecessary to use the pyramid or Merkaba processes once one has a grasp of further concepts of advanced consciousness and access to higher realms. Exercises toward that higher consciousness will be described later in this book. The purpose of these exercises is for you to gain an understanding of yourself beyond the physical self that you currently perceive.

By doing these exercises, you are consciously participating as a part of the Universal process. You have maintained awareness of yourself as a consciousness, as a human being and as a part of the living Universe. You are beginning to understand a little bit about multi-dimensionality and the fact that you are not restricted to the body that you inhabit nor the world in which you live. You are beginning to step out of the box and into greater realities. Once you have begun to grasp multi-dimensional awareness, all of your perceptions of reality begin to change. Your value system will change as well, for without the everyday dramatics that we apply to our third dimensional realities, the world and all that it is it takes on a whole new meaning. We. Are. The. One.

Chapter Four
Working Within the Holographic Reality

We now have an understanding of how the universe works and why it works, and we have experienced the pyramid exercises, taking the first steps outside of this local reality. How do we apply this to our everyday experience? After all, what good is having a bunch of information without knowing what to do with it? We are about to explore taking our consciousness farther out into other realities.

By first understanding the process and then participating in the creation of our own reality, we begin to take back our power as whole and perfect beings of Light. We become capable of seeing past the illusions that are created in this world every minute of every day. We can begin to remember what we have always known but have forgotten how to access.

In the first chapter of this book, we learned how the Universe is constructed with the particulates and the null zones. We learned that from there, all planes of reality and existence were created. As above so below — everything is constructed in the same format. We learned later that our consciousness exists in many realities at once.

How do we communicate with our other aspects? How do we work in tandem with our other selves to fine tune our abilities toward a state of wholeness and one great experience rather than as fractured beings? By utilizing the tools contained in this chapter alone, we may create within ourselves an entirely new environment of conscious awareness.

Later in this chapter we will learn how to work outside our physical bodies in a way that is not only safe, but allows us to maintain awareness of our physical, third-dimensional selves while we learn and work within other realities. This is our Gamma Consciousness.

We will learn how to multi-facet ourselves toward being in and aware of many realities simultaneously, while being at once both the observer and the practitioner.

Why would we want to do this? Mostly to know that we have other choices. How to be the creators of our own realities. To realize unequivocally that we are the Masters of our own existence. To take the power that is ours and use it toward creating a greater reality within ourselves, our environment, our world. To remember the Truth.

The Seventh Sense™

We know that as human beings we utilize the five senses of hearing, seeing, touch, taste and smell. Those senses serve us well in our local environment but are related primarily to our third-dimensional, physical experience.

Beyond our five basic senses, many of us experience a connection with our sixth sense, our intuitive nature. With this intuition we are capable of gaining insight about situations, people, places or events that have either occurred or are about to happen. These insights come in flashes of visions or feelings. They come as sudden thoughts or in many other ways, depending upon how we as individuals perceive our world.

Some of us perceive visually while others have a sense or a knowing about things. Some of us feel the world without the visual enhancements. Our sixth sense works with intangible perceptual experiences and remains generally limited to sensing information about events within our local reality, the third dimension or just beyond, into the immediate afterlife.

Our Seventh Sense™ takes us much farther. By attaining Gamma Consciousness, we move into *multi-dimensional reality*. With our Seventh Sense™ we operate wholly as a consciousness which functions separately from our physical bodies. We become free of the dense physicality that we inhabit.

Our Seventh Sense™ allows us to take our consciousness as pure energy into the null zones to travel anywhere, anytime, any place within the entirety of creation.

Different from all of our other senses, the Seventh Sense™ also allows us to interactively participate with full sensory awareness within those other locales.

Consciously from within our Seventh Sense™, we remain aware of who we are third dimensionally as we explore other dimensional realms. We become completely aware of the other realities, times, places and events that we visit... with practice, all at the same time!

This multi-faceted way of being is the perfect tool for learning. Imagine taking our consciousness right into the memory banks of the universe! There, we can learn as much or as little about anything or any subject we desire. From the Seventh Sense™ we are operating as pure and conscious energy. Therefore, when we access these information banks as pure energy, the force contained within the universal memory intermingles with our energy and we have instant and complete awareness of whatever subject we desired to access. Basically, we become infused with knowledge.

Using the Seventh Sense™ for healing self and others offers entirely new avenues for wellness in every direction. Since the Seventh Sense™ allows access to all levels of existence, a healer can travel ethereally and other-dimensionally, accessing and repairing affectations on other dimensional planes of being that may be affecting the subject's third-dimensional existence in the here and now.

The Seventh Sense™ offers no limitations to what can be experienced in the inner and outer realms, or of the possibilities that can be gained from those experiences. Using the Seventh Sense™, we see ourselves as holograms in other realities as we reflect the light of our being into the vibrations of those realities. In these alternate realities we are able to see, feel, hear, taste, smell and intuit wherever we travel. Of course this does take practice!

But how do we access our Seventh Sense™? Later in this chapter we will learn the Movement to Spirit™ exercise that helps us gain access to the other dimensional realms, but first, a bit of explanation.

The Science of Consciousness

Accessing the Seventh Sense™ requires the instigation of Gamma brain wave activity. An exercise to facilitate the onset of Gamma Consciousness are contained later in this book.

We have many different levels of brain wave activity, each serving a particular purpose in our functioning. For example, we use Delta brain waves when we sleep, Alpha brain waves for relaxation, and Theta brain waves when we meditate. Sixth sense activities occur mostly when we have accessed our Theta brain waves.

At this point in human evolution we use very little of our brain functioning... somewhere under ten percent. When we instigate Gamma brain wave functioning, the Gamma waves act as a unifier to the electrical and electro-magnetic circuitry within our brains. The Gamma waves move outward from the center of our brain in a uniform fashion, uniting parts of the brain that have not ever worked together in our current states of consciousness. Upon unification of electrical and electro-magnetic functioning, an interesting thing happens. We immediately leap into higher consciousness. We let go of lower brain wave functioning and gain the freedom to use our Seventh Sense™ unhindered! We awaken to multi-dimensional awareness.

There are three levels of Gamma brain wave functioning. Each level is triggered within an area of the brain based upon the golden ratio, or relationships of the mathematical value of phi, which create a spiral. This geometric formation is the basis for the design and layout of sacred sites around the world as well as in nature. In fact,

Every sacred site in the world that is built with the golden ratio is a demonstration of our highest state of consciousness!

Remember from Chapter One that the universe is constructed based upon the arrangement of Light in the form of pyramids and that each pyramid contains a spiral? And from Chapter Seven that each pyramid represents the true trinity? Consciousness is based upon that very construct!

The golden ratio, or spiral formation is demonstrated mathematically by Fibonacci sequence. The Fibonacci sequence is a formula which is based upon a number sequence beginning with zero and each following number being the sum of the two preceding numbers. For example:

$0+1=1$, $1+1=2$, $2+1=3$, $3+2=5$, $5+3=8$..... And so the numbers in the sequence begin to look like this:

0, 1, 1, 2, 3, 5, 8, 13, 21, 34, 55.... And so on. This sequence moves outward into infinity.

In addition, dividing each number in the Fibonacci series by the number which precedes it produces a ratio which stabilizes at about 1.618034, or phi, which is the golden ratio.

Within our brains, the golden spiral is centered at the pineal gland and also incorporates the pituitary gland and the hypothalamus. As the spiral moves outward, it coils across the corpus callosum within the central brain area.

The corpus callosum is an area within the central brain that has, by evolutionary processes, become denser in form than its original biological formation. In the same way that the matter became denser, so did the energies within the structure.

In our current state of evolution, the energies within the central brain and particularly the corpus callosum are restructuring toward a looser formation. With this new energetic arrangement, Gamma brain waves, once initiated, easily penetrate outwardly in a spiral motion, having originated in the area of the pineal gland. With the new energetic structuring there will be noticeable biological changes of the corpus callosum.

As these energetic and physical changes occur, we become able to let go of our perceived connection between body and consciousness, moving into our aspects of higher consciousness all the way into multi-dimensional reality.

Practically applied within brain matter and functioning, the golden spiral looks much like Figure 12:

Figure 12: The Golden Spiral as Related to the Brain

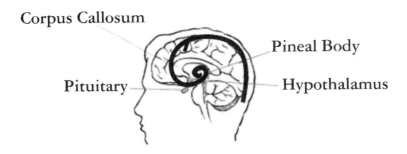

Each of the three levels of Gamma brain wave function takes us to a higher state of consciousness. The first level is *Initiation*. The Initiation level is accessed at the end of the widest point of the spiral. When accessing the initiation phase of Gamma wave activity, we begin to access higher consciousness and experience initial awareness of other realities. We may see or experience glimpses of other realities, colors, geometric shapes, or other forms of living energy.

The second level of Gamma wave functioning is accessed at the crest of the spiral, the widest part of the exterior curve. This level is called *Communion*. During the Communion phase, one may actually interact within other dimensional realms while experiencing a full range of senses. It is within this level of functioning that the Seventh Sense™ becomes fully operational and may be utilized as described earlier in this chapter.

The third level of Gamma brain wave activity is the *Ascension point* which is located at the smallest point of the spiral. It is from this extremely high place of functioning that we are able to directly and consciously ascend into the Light with or without our physical bodies. This is a level of awareness that only Masters throughout history have achieved, but is possible for anyone to experience.

The actual relationships between Gamma brain wave instigation points as related to the golden ratio within the brain are represented in the diagram in Figure 13:

Figure 13: Three Levels of Gamma Consciousness

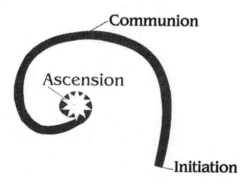

As we begin to access Gamma Brain waves within ourselves, the Initiation point is at the beginning of the spiral which is reflected by the Fibonacci sequence. (As we learned in Chapter One, that spiral is also the base of a pyramid!) The Communion point is at the wide center point of the spiral (in the pyramid, this was the area where we combined the upright and inverted pyramids, forming a relationship between ourselves and the universal mind), and the Ascension point is at the apex of the spiral, the same as that of tip of the pyramid.

What happens to our perceptions of realities when we begin to access and interact within these higher stages of awareness? Reality begins to be quite a bit different. Our value systems begin to change dramatically because we begin to understand that the drama and trauma that we experience in our daily lives means nothing when we begin to actively participate within the One...

The Genetic Connection

There is much speculation about how DNA, our genetic material that is formed of segments and organized in a spiraled double helix, is related to consciousness. As with our brains, very little of our DNA is active.

What is the relationship of our DNA to consciousness? When we access the Gamma brainwave state, certain changes occur within our bodies. The electrical and electromagnetic relationships within us change. Our brains, operating with a new unified electromagnetic state, begin sending new and different signals to us both energetically and chemically. As this occurs, our bodies respond.

The electrical impulses which initiate response from one segment of our DNA to the next respond to the new and unified signal patterns from within the brain by changing their electrical patterning of communication along the double helix.

The electrical impulses which communicate information from one DNA strand and segment to the next begin to arc, skipping the usual paths of communication and corresponding with other segments of DNA that had previously remained dormant. As this arcing occurs, new relationships within our bodies are developed.

The new relationships among our DNA segments and strands signal our brains that a new physiological environment has occurred. In turn, our brains begin to release chemicals in different ratios than are released during our normal daily activities. We often become blissful and euphoric.

The new electrical and electro-magnetic relationships within our bodies create an entirely different type of field of energy within us. The energy that we begin to experience is operating in a highly unified fashion. In that alliance, our field of energy is literally becoming a unified field of energy, of Light. We begin to function in the same way that the particulates and null zones function!

As our energetic fields unify, our vibrational rates change and our energies are emitted at higher frequencies. Our bodies begin to harmonize physically in a set of harmonics that match the individual universal identifiers which are the sum of all of the harmonies contained within our particulates.

In that moment, our bodies and our consciousness become one.

When this occurs, our consciousness awakens to the recognition of self. No longer sensing limitations, the consciousness begins to once again travel freely within the universal process. Our DNA acts as a crystallized liquid with no gaps in the synapses of communication. We begin to function as the One.

Cosmic Education – A Personal Experience

To best describe some of the possibilities that are available to us when we attain higher consciousness into the Gamma state and our Seventh Sense™, I can think of no better way than to tell you a part of my own story.

Early in my transition from the illusions of everyday existence I learned that I had to give myself permission to live my life as I am, not as others would have me. Up to that point in my life I had lived and judged myself based upon everything that I thought others expected of me. I was trying to prove my worthiness to a world that wasn't even paying attention. This new way had to be about me, what *I* wanted and needed, or so I thought...

I knew that within me were gifts that had yet to be recognized and explored. I had hidden them from myself and others for most of my life. The only way that I would be free to embark on this new journey was to accept myself and all that I am with none of the previous perceptions that I was anything less than perfect. Somehow I knew that if I were going to learn anything at all, I had to be free of all of the encumbrances that I had allowed in my life and find the courage and the freedom to emerge from all that had kept me from soaring toward the self that longed to get free.

Basically, I had to accept the assignment of my own existence. The responsibility of this seemed immense but in actuality my acceptance became the freedom to fly.

Once I embraced myself and my new horizons my consciousness began to open quickly — much faster than I could comprehend or had anticipated. I quickly outgrew the experience and knowledge of every person who was accessible to me at that time. My reality was taking quantum leaps and there seemed to be no limitations as to how far I could go. Trying to mentally understand the exciting awareness that was growing within me only led to confusion. Worse, thinking about everything often stopped the process completely. None of the old rules applied, so I decided to give up all attempts to control my journey and, as I said at the time, "let Spirit be my teacher"

And boy, did Spirit teach me!

I continue to laughingly say that you must be careful what you ask for! From one passionate moment of asking for what I thought I needed, my life, my reality, my heart became forever changed.

In all of the experiences that followed, I realized that what I needed was nothing. I had everything. I had simply forgotten how to recognize that. All of the answers that I sought had been right there inside me all along!

My new adventure took me into realities far beyond imagination. At times what I experienced was both inconceivable and emotionally overwhelming, but I didn't stop. Instead, I asked for more!

The trick all along has been to remember that what I have gained and learned is never about me or what I have become able to do, but rather to remember that the source of my knowledge, my gifts, is much greater than me. I became a willing conduit for the greater whole.

Part of my lesson was to discover humility. In many ways, it was about setting aside my competitive nature while learning to proceed from my most secret vulnerabilities. At first I felt raw and exposed, but in a while as I became filled with what I later recognized as *real* unconditional love (that which is a state of grace, not an emotional experience!), I began to realize that nothing that

I had ever deemed important *was*. My value system changed completely.

I also learned that expectations are pitfalls. When I expected an experience to be a certain way, it never was. I had to trust that whatever was next would be okay and that I would learn exactly what was needed. I learned that expectations are limitations that set up an environment for disappointment or failure.

Movement to Spirit™ came about out of pure desperation to understand what was happening to me. I had begun to feel different types of energy in my hands and fingers. Living energies in my hands. Little squiggly spirals in my fingers that changed upon certain types of stimulation. Other energies that were affecting my body and I didn't know what to do with all of it.

Every day I gave myself time to explore what I was feeling, yet no answers came. I was, I felt, cosmically constipated. Nothing I could think of helped me past my state of ethereal "stuckness". One morning out of pure frustration I stood in my living room with a heart full of passion, music playing, and I *begged* (I know, it isn't very pretty to think about, but remember, I was desperate) for help. I begged *out loud* to no one in particular.... "Teach me!"

With the music playing I closed my eyes and found the primary energy between my hands. I began to move my hands further apart, concentrating only on the energy. I had no expectations mostly because I had no experience with this kind of thing.

I began to move my hands apart while I concentrated on the energy between them and I naturally began to sway with the music. As I moved with the music, the energy got bigger. I could feel things stirring inside of me. I could feel that I was opening from the inside out and it felt fantastic.

And so I kept doing it. I began to push the energy away from me then pull it back, over my head and along my body, feeling the energies wash over me. I noticed that when I did, the energetic relationships both inside and around me changed. I moved the energy in other ways, and one morning, with my hands palm up and level with my hips an arc of energy flew over my head, and *it was alive*! The arc of energy was living, moving color. It seemed that the force that I was working with was not only real but something that I could see and control.

Excited about this inkling of progress, I set out to see what was next. I did the exercise anywhere from ten minutes to an hour each morning. I knew that seeing the living dynamics of energy was magnificent to say the least, but what good was it if I didn't know what to do with it? I wanted more.

As I worked I asked.... Ok, so I pleaded, (you have to remember that I had no one else to query!) "Show me more! How can I be of service with what I am being given...? Please...! Show me more!"

And did they ever show me! Remember the old adage "be careful what you ask for"? I found out unequivocally what that means...

I got the help I asked for but never in a way I expected! That morning as I explored living energy through movement and music, much to my shock and surprise, as I was going through the motions, I looked up with my etheric eyes, and there standing before me was a most beautiful being. He was a hologram. He manifested to me as a young man, but appeared to be from somewhere in distant history, an ancient one to be sure.

My guest wore robes of crimson lined and bordered with gold. He had been standing there waiting for me to notice him but I was so busy trying to get it that I nearly missed him! Of course I nearly jumped out of my skin when I saw him! When I did, he disappeared. Although I had a million questions, I set them aside, doing everything in my power to preserve the state in which I had just been. I shook off my surprise, collected myself and invited him back. Amazingly, he returned.

This was the beginning of an incredible relationship.

First and foremost, I wanted to make certain that I was working with someone who was of the Light, not some trickster who might lead me astray in my process. After determining that he was of Light, I asked him what he had come to teach me. In response he began to move, just as I had been moving during my exercises with the energy. His hands filled with light in different colors and shapes, and that light was doing fantastic things...Both the colors and intensities changed. As my holographic friend moved, the light became many things, also holographic. He proved himself a Master of the unimaginable. Some of the objects that materialized looked very solid while others were almost too unbearably bright to behold.

Understanding that this breathtaking Master had come to teach me, I began to mimic his moves. Whatever he did, I did the same. As he moved for me, with me, I began to experience within my hands similar changes in the energies that he was creating for me to see within his own hands.

Exquisite arrays of living color seemed to come alive at his silent command. Geometric shapes and combinations of shapes created of color and light appeared, changed and went. Objects seemed to materialize out of nowhere. The more I practiced, the better I felt. I began to feel as if I were glowing from the inside out.

As I followed the Master each morning, my heart opened more fully. The joy within me infiltrated every moment of every day. I had more energy than I knew what to do with. Still, I continued to do the movement exercise each morning.

This first Master did not stay for too many sessions. Quickly I was brought to another reality. One morning as magically as he came, my wonderful teacher had gone. I found that my reality had shifted to just outside a courtyard that looked like an ancient place. Cobblestones covered the ground. There was a stone archway which led into the courtyard where I could see other people milling about, but I wasn't allowed to enter. I had a sense that this was a place of learning, and was reminded of the ancient Greeks who used to gather as apprentices to the various Masters.

(In that moment I realized that holographic sight was just like my own physical sight. I was using my etheric vision, working with my eyes closed, yet if I turned my head in either direction I saw an extension of the scene that was happening in front of me. Peripheral holography! I also realized that while I was experiencing this new reality I was still conscious of my three-dimensional self. Without realizing it, I had become multi-dimensionally aware!)

My lessons in this new venue began in front of the archway. To my left there was a new Master sitting on the sideline. He was old and wizened with long silver hair and an unkempt beard that fell to his chest. His protruding belly made a perfect resting place for his chubby hands and sometimes his chin as he dozed, waiting for me to progress with the exercises that he gave. This Master felt strong and certain of himself, and not a little impatient with me. He seemed preoccupied with a myriad of otherworldly things. Between us rested a small square wooden table with inlays of malachite, azurite and other colorful stones in a strange and beautiful array of shapes and patterns. Somehow the design seemed familiar to me but I have not yet placed it...

As I looked at him, the Master indicated for me to begin.

And so I did. I began to move in the same way that the first Master had shown me. One of the things that the first Master had often done was to bring the energy to a crescendo as he raised his hands high in front of himself. As his hands rose, the power of the light with in his hands seemed to magnify. So I did that for the new Master. I called the light into my hands and watched it come to life. Raising my arms slowly, in my heart and soul I became the energy in my hands. The light flared out and something formed in my hands... a small carved object! It was unlike anything I had ever seen before! After examining the object, I brought it down carefully and put it on the Master's table.

He quietly (barely it seemed) acknowledged my accomplishment. I started to feel unnoticed, like a kid in class with his hand was raised and someone else was called upon for the answer... but then I realized that this process was about *my* learning, not *the Master's* approval.

We worked together for many days as I learned how to create realities out of the energies with which I was working. I was often brought to nearly total emotional overwhelm during the time that I worked with this Master. My abilities improved toward creating changes in reality. One morning after raising my hands into the light, as I lowered them back toward myself I discovered a white dove between my hands. I could feel its warmth, its heartbeat against my palms. I could smell its dander, feel its breath as it nervously nestled between my hands. In one respect the bird seemed to be a mere hologram, but in every other respect, it was as alive as I was.

I stood there with tears running down both of my faces — my third-dimensional self and the one who was working with the Master in the courtyard. I felt the life force of this little creature growing in my hands. Bringing the dove close to my chest, I felt my heart reach into it. Savoring the moment, I raised my hands and let him fly away. And fly away he did. He lifted up and out of my hands and became a dove of pure white Light, hovering just beyond me in the distance. The dove remained as I completed my session that morning.

A few days later just as I began my morning lessons with the Master, a young man came and tapped me on the shoulder. (Yes, I actually felt it). "Can't you see I am studying?" I said. "Please don't bother me right now." (Thinking back on this I realize that this was the first time I could hear what was being said to me.) The youth continued his attempts to get my attention by telling me that I was being summoned and that I had to go with him right away. The third time he asked, I acquiesced. I followed the young man down a dirt footpath and soon we came to a place that I had not seen before.

The place was a grotto of sorts, carved naturally of stone with an overhang that served as a shelter. As my eyes adjusted to the darker environment, I realized that the White Brotherhood stood there in a circle! (The White Brotherhood is a group of Light-oriented etheric beings who assist in healing, sacred learning and many other aspects of working from one dimension to another.) Just to the right of the circle stood yet another Master. He was also dressed in the white robes of the Brotherhood.

This Master's medium brown hair cascaded below his shoulders. His eyes were dark and penetrating yet held some spark of amusement as he looked at me. Wordlessly with those eyes he summoned me before him. I tried to tell him that I had work to do, that I needed to get back to my studies, but he cut me off with a glance.

In his hands the new Master held a sword with the tip down. I knelt before him and he touched the sword to my shoulders and placed his right hand on the crown of my head, holding it there. I could feel the power of his touch. The energy of him was strong with a force I had not felt before.

Somehow I still wasn't grasping the importance of the moment. As the ceremony finished, I thanked the Master and began to walk away, impatiently heading back to my studies. Whatever the ceremony was, it seemed that I had much more learning to do and I was anxious to return to my lessons. The Master of my initiation looked at me with an odd bit of exasperation as I left. He reminded me of a patient father watching a child learn the hard way.

I tried to return to the courtyard. It was impossible. Only then did I realize that I had graduated! I had successfully learned the skills that had come to me and I had moved beyond the teachings of the wizened one at the archway. It was once again time to begin a new reality... and a new set of lessons.

This became a pattern over time. With each initiation to a higher place of learning, I became unable to go back to previous lessons or venue. I learned very quickly that I had better be paying attention!

The next place my reality took me was to a chamber of healing. This chamber was to be one of many. This place was so ancient that it was beyond any recorded history or even myth of history. It was beyond what I already knew of Lemuria and of Atlantis. This was from what I was told was the "before time".

There was a table in the new chamber that was made of a substance that I didn't recognize. Not really metal, not really stone. The Master who met me there was lined with age and exuded not only wisdom but a confidence and strength of knowledge. This was a wise one. Not that the others weren't, but this Master oozed the ancient ways. And he did it with unflappable confidence. I had a sense that this Master was the embodiment of everything he had come to teach me.

I stepped up to the table next to the Master. Right about the same time, I realized that I was also observing us from about twenty feet away. When I turned around and looked I could see myself. The perspective changed back and forth several times as the me with the Master looked at the me who was watching and the me who was watching looked at the me with the Master. This was getting complicated. There were two of me! Wait! NO! Three! The earthly me was aware of everything as well! Had I fractionalized? How was all of this possible? I *seemed* to be okay. I felt like myself as I checked here, there, in all three places...

Determined to avoid further confusion I turned my attention to the Master before me. The long robe he wore was so blue it was nearly purple. It rippled down his long length as if nothing else in any world would fit him. The robe reflected light as he moved, almost as if *he was* the embodiment of light. As I stepped up to the table, I looked down toward where I expected my hands to be and much to my surprise, what I saw were the arms and hands of the Master! He had stepped into me to guide me in the lesson. In that moment, we were one.

The Master conjoined with me energetically as a living guide who in some sense controlled my every movement and heightened the sensations that I was experiencing. The part of me who was watching from a distance saw that when the Master stepped in to guide me, a holographic pyramid of energy had surrounded the area in which we were working, a perfect field of energy from within to call any array of energies.

We were working in an environment of perfection. The holographic pyramid radiated a light golden glow and somehow, as I learned from this Master, I began to know not just one movement, not just one technique, but a complete cognizance of many aspects of holographic energy healing all at once! Incredible! I got the how's and the why's in such a form that it would have been impossible to describe how I was learning in mere words. He was infusing me with knowledge!

As I advanced with this Master, he began to show me how to look beyond the local reality to yet another healing chamber where, when a body was levitated, it would turn slowly, allowing for a diagnosis of malfunctioning of the energy system and occasionally the organs. It was fascinating to say the least. Like a sponge I absorbed the teachings.

There were times when I worked with this Master that I would begin my movement exercise in the morning and suddenly a holographic representation of a human being whom I knew or had heard of and who was having health issues, would materialize before me. The presenting bodies levitated just as in the second healing chamber I described above, and as they did, I could see where there were irregularities within and around them.

These types of displays became the norm for a while. Upon levitation, the bodies would slowly spin and within the body I would be shown malfunctioning energy patterns. These bodies and their malfunctions were presented as teaching tools to show me how to apply what I was learning to my third dimensional reality. I began to repair the anomalies that I saw by learning to transmute the energies. This, to me, was the ultimate alchemic process — changing the form of one reality to another to effect healing. In this case, from the dysfunction of illness to healing and wellness.

In later lessons, as I did the movement and energy work, Jesus stood before me and guided me in certain aspects of what I was learning. He worked differently, as a rule, than the other Masters had, standing there, and emanating everything that I needed to know while he looked into my eyes. Somehow I understood completely.

Instead of telepathically, Jesus taught me energetically. What he gave me became a part of me that I could recall at will. Occasionally he would "step in" as the other Master had done and when he did, if I had to find one word to describe the feeling, it would be balance. Balance of every aspect of myself inside and out. *Being* the One.

(Jesus often comes to healing sessions that I do with myself and others, even now. Throughout my learning process and for many, many years, he has been with me. There are no words to describe the experience of Him or the love that comes through Him when he is present.)

Ultimately there were other Masters, other lessons, and I graduated several more times. I was taught how to access other times and places. One of the most profound experiences I had was when I asked to experience the crucifixion of Jesus. I found myself accompanying him on his final walk toward impending death and sharing both energetically and physically the expression of his pain as each nail was hammered into his body.

Somehow I hovered near him as he anguished upon the cross, gently cupping his face with my hand, feeling the sweat of his pain running down my hands as I touched him. As I stroked his face I felt enormous waves of love. I accompanied him through the burial process as three women washed and then anointed Jesus with what looked and felt like a thick olive oil-based substance. It was fragrant with a rich combination of scents.

When the preparations were complete, Jesus was wrapped in a white cloth and the tomb was sealed. My journey stopped there and at the time I wondered why I was not allowed to complete the journey through the resurrection. It dawned on me later that if I were present for the resurrection, as I was exposed to the Light I would have ascended myself, and it was not time for me to do that just yet. Being present for such a series of events brought me to my knees. I was in tears for hours. The passion and compassion was more expansive than anything I had yet experienced. I have to admit that I was emotionally wasted after that one.

There have been countless other lessons. One afternoon when I had time to sit and experience whatever came next, I was immediately taken through several realities in time. Different millennia — one, then the next, and the next. I felt as if I had been boomeranged through times and realities one after the other and did not know how to control the experience. I felt as if my space-time gyroscope was out of whack as I went from one scene to another. Each place and time assaulted my perceptions with tactile experiences, odors, scents, partial glimpses of scenes and events that did not seem rational to my thinking self. What I witnessed in those moments went from base to the ridiculous as my logical mind could not comprehend.

Somehow my reality survived. Ultimately in that particular expedition, I ended up watching another Master from a distance as he raised his hands of Light. His robes were of shades of light purple. His shiny black hair and closely trimmed beard shone dark against his porcelain skin. This Master radiated peace and a fullness of wisdom in a way I had not yet experienced. *There was so much love.* I knew in that instant what I was supposed to do.

I went over and put my arms around the Master's waist... and... I... *stepped into... him*! Immediately he and I were the same. One. As soon as this occurred, the scene changed and I found myself in a dark room with him. A chamber of sorts. Within his hands the Master held a golden chalice which had been etched with symbols, all in a spiral fashion the full length of the stem. The Master was moving the chalice carefully in a small circular way. I looked inside of the cup and there inside was not wine, not water, but liquid light!

"Drink of this" the Master said. And so I did. From that moment forward my life has never been the same. Synchronicities began to happen in the most astounding ways. Instant manifestation occurred with little to no effort. In all my heart, I know that this was my true ordination. I had become the Spirit who was my teacher.

There have been countless other experiences like the ones I have just described. There is still so much to learn. I have laughed and I have cried, even briefly questioned my rationality. Was all of this real? Was I creating it all in my imagination? I came to the unquestionable conclusion that yes, it is all real and no, I hadn't made any of it up. What I learned I applied within my third-dimensional world, to assist in the healing and teaching of others — often with phenomenal results.

The point is that there are in fact realities beyond the here and now that have everything to teach us if we choose to experience them.

It comes down to how far we want to go and what we mean to do with what we have learned. And, in all honesty, the purity and selflessness with which we ask for what we need.

This kind of knowledge is not for the keeping. It is for the telling, the showing, and the miraculous changes that can be achieved in our spirits as well as in our lives and the lives of others. Wisdom is found in that sharing.

We can take this type of experience as far as we wish from simple awareness to complete participation within the other realities. Of course, to do that means that we have to step out of the secure illusions of our boxes and give ourselves the freedom to experience the worlds beyond... It is always our choice.

Getting There – About Movement to Spirit™

As promised, Movement to Spirit™ is an exercise that assists us to leap to Gamma Consciousness. This process naturally developed as I moved with music and worked with the energies within and around me and became one of the largest factors in my awakening to other realities. Since I had asked Spirit to teach me, and this was the avenue to greater realities for me, I called this process "Movement to Spirit™".

I have taught this exercise to groups both large and small in cities all over the United States and New Zealand. Many who have attended this workshop for the first time have had amazing results. Some have opened to higher awareness almost immediately, while others have seen colors when they had never seen them before. Other people have had huge openings of the heart, experiencing releases of emotional withholdings. A few have even seen or felt the touch of the Masters.

I would like to share this process to you now...

But first, a few words of caution. This technique really works. It seems very simple and it is. It is fun and even good for you in a lot of ways. On the other hand, if you do this exercise without taking time to assimilate what you are learning, your reality may leap quickly far beyond what you are able to comprehend. Your rational self can only take so much change at once, so take a few days off now and then to give yourself time to integrate the energies with which you are working. It is best not to dwell within your mind about what you experience while doing Movement to Spirit™ — rather to allow your opening to unfold as it is given.

This process incorporates the use of many high frequency energies which are very different than what you experience on an everyday basis.

Using these energies to any extreme until you are physically adapted to them can cause physiological changes within your body. Overuse of this process may cause certain mineral depletion in your body or uncomfortable physical symptoms. Give yourself time to adapt.

If necessary, supplementing your diet with magnesium or a calcium-magnesium supplement will assist with the changes that working with these energies may cause within your body. (Of course, if you do choose to supplement, please consider consulting your health care professional!)

Remember that whatever you gain from doing this exercise is your experience. Each person will gain awareness based upon the regularity of this exercise, readiness to bring in change and willingness to accept those changes. What is experienced and at what rate is also dependant upon the level of vibration from which you are beginning.

Be careful what you are thinking about as you work with energy in this exercise. Instant manifestation has been known to occur. Do not ever begin this exercise with negative feelings or emotions — rather from a perspective of living creativity.

You are in total and complete control of your experience. You may choose to stop or encounter more at any time you wish, simply by asking. You see, by doing this exercise you are not waiting for something to come along and change you, you are participating in your own process of change!

You are creating an environment from which your consciousness may springboard into change and other realities. Since this is your creation, you have the ability to move within that creation at whatever rate of acceleration is comfortable for you.

If at any time you find yourself uncomfortable, simply stop doing the exercise.

The best way to practice Movement to Spirit™ is in a step-by-step process so that you can get a good feel for what you are experiencing. Each step, while very simple, brings about new awareness.

As you become more and more comfortable with each step, you will probably want to begin combining the steps into one fluid exercise of movement. I have laughingly called this process my own personal brand of Tai Chi!

Movement to Spirit™

Step One: Find some music that moves your heart. You know... the kind that makes you feel all big inside, emotional. It is best not to use hemi-sync (brainwave balancing) music or music that has words when you first begin. Most brain wave music will actually keep you from experiencing the leap to Gamma state. Words carry energy of their own due to the tones and meanings behind the words and therefore make the music more complex.

Music becomes an actual part of you while you are listening to it. As the music plays, it is released into the environment as the energy of sound. That energy signals the particulates within your body to temporarily restructure, allowing the particulates of the music to intertwine with yours. In these moments you become changed. You and the music are, in a way, sharing space. This is why music has such great emotional effect (see Figure 14).When you are ready, begin playing the music.

Step Two: With your eyes closed, hold your hands out in front of you, side by side (pinkie side down), with the palms facing each other (like you see people do when they pray), but without letting your hands touch. Hold your hands just close enough together that you can feel the warm energy between them. This is your own life force, the one that interrelates universally.

Move your hands apart slowly until you can still barely feel the energy but haven't lost awareness of it. It may take some people a little bit longer to find the energy than others. This is not unusual if you have never worked with energy before. Be patient with yourself. Once you have found the energy and are comfortable, you are ready to begin.

Figure 14: The Effects of Music, Movement and Energy

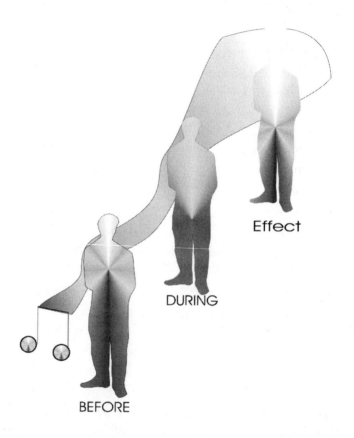

Effect

DURING

BEFORE

As the energy of music moves through our energy fields, the musical energy progresses through the color spectrum. As it does, our particulates temporarily harmonize with the energy of the music. As these changes occur, our particulates part in mathematical increments to allow a clear passage of energy not only through our bodies but our brains. This allows for the unification of our brain waves into the Gamma state which in turn connects us to the universal mind.

Step Three: As the music plays, and with your eyes remaining closed, begin to move your body and your arms, allowing your hands to remain apart. Sway gently with the rhythm of the music. It is okay to move your feet if you like. Focus on the energy that is between your hands. Begin to move your hands farther apart. What happens to the energy when you do this? Does it get smaller? Larger? More intense? Does the feeling change in any other way? Be aware of what is happening with the energy that you are experiencing. Keep your eyes closed and enjoy the experience of the energy changes.

Note: As you continue with this exercise, it is vitally important that you remember to breathe! Your breath is what assists the energy as it flows through your body. It cleanses you, nourishes you and maintains your internal balance.

You may begin to feel extremely emotional during this exercise. That is fine. It is a natural part of the opening process. As you begin to raise your consciousness, your frequencies, your vibrational rate also begins to rise. As it does, your body begins to release certain chemicals that trigger the release of emotional stuff that you have tucked away in your body. Breathe through the feelings and let the tears or other emotions flow if they come. Know that you are becoming of the perfection that you are...

Step Four: As the music continues to play, keep your eyes closed, focusing on the energy between your hands just as you have done in the previous steps. Now, as you have become more comfortable with this process, begin to move more freely. Push the energy outward; let your hands spread farther apart as you do. It is okay if you change your hand positions as long as you continue to be aware of the energy with which you are working.

Pull the energy back toward yourself. How does this feel? Is it different than when you push the energy away? As you pull the energy back toward you, try bringing it down over your head and down your body. Does this change how you feel? What is your sense? Are you becoming different inside with each movement? Is your sensitivity to your environment becoming more acute?

Note: As you begin to advance the steps of this exercise, you may experience some pain in certain areas of your body. The areas which are exhibiting pain are telling you that you have an energy blockage in that area. To remove the blockage, deliberately breathe into the painful area, imagining that your breath is carrying the blockage out of your body as you exhale.

Step Five: As the music continues to play, keep your eyes closed, focusing on the energy between your hands just as you have done in the previous steps. This time as you move, reach as far above your head as you can, bringing the energies down slowly over your head and your body (not touching yourself). Can you feel the subtle changes as you move your hands downward? Now, reach down in front of your feet. Bring the energies of the earth up your legs, your body, and over your head. How do these energies feel different from the ones you brought in from above?

Step Six: As the music continues to play, keep your eyes closed, focusing on the energy between your hands just as you have done in the previous step. With a hand palm up at the level of each hip, pull energy up your sides (still not touching). As you move your hands upward, breathe inwardly. Do you feel the flow of energy traveling from one chakra center to the next? Can you feel your kundalini, the energy that moves up your energetic center, awakening? What happens when you deliberately breathe as you move your body, your hands? Does your breath change how the energy feels within or around you?

Step Seven: As the music continues to play, keep your eyes closed, focusing on the energy between your hands just as you have done in the previous step. Begin to move your body and your hands freely as you are guided. Listen to your body and allow yourself to move with the motion that it desires. Do not feel as if you must remain in one place. It's okay to move your feet!

Move as you will, experiencing the energies as you change position and direction. What effect does direction have on how you perceive the energies? Is there a difference from one direction to another? Try facing each of the cardinal directions, i.e. North, South, East, and West. Does the direction you are facing change the way the energy feels? Allow yourself to naturally move in any way you desire.

The only rules are that you continue to play the music, focus only on the energy that you are working with, and remember to breathe. Remember, this is your experience. Only you will know what movement is most beneficial to you!

This exercise can be done daily for a few minutes or up to an hour as you get stronger. I would not recommend that you do this any more often than that even though it feels awesome. There are changes that are occurring physiologically and energetically within you and around you that will cause you to open in consciousness too quickly if you do this exercise too often. You may deplete minerals that are important to your body.

You may also become overcharged with energy. If this occurs, stop the exercise for a few days and do whatever works best for you to become grounded again. Put your hands in the dirt outside, eat a piece of chocolate, run cold water on your wrists, or even hug a tree. Whatever works for you so that you become grounded and feel completely in your body. It is very easy to become addicted to the sensations that are created by doing this exercise. Remember that even though the physical sensations are incredibly wonderful, they are not what this is about. Rather, this is to assist you toward opening to a higher state of conscious awareness.

The Awakening process is an amazing experience. It requires an open heart and mind as well as the willingness to step into new and higher realities. Remember, you get what you ask for! This exercise will take you as far as you want to go. Your consciousness will open farther and farther depending upon how dedicated you are to the process. It is entirely up to you how far to take this. Use discretion and please, be careful not to over do it! Perhaps we will meet in one of the many dimensions... Enjoy the ride!

Section Two

How Our Universal Relationships Work

Chapter Five
Understanding Our Life Purpose

In my private practice, the most frequently asked question is "What is my Life Purpose?" The answer is simple:

Every moment that we exist we are fulfilling our purpose.

Every interaction that we have, every set of circumstances in which we participate, and every bit of energy that we give or receive in that interaction changes the world forever.

The preceding statement may sound a bit dramatic but it is true. In every situation we encounter, we contribute not only through our actions, thoughts and words, but energetically as well. The energy with which we communicate becomes exchanged with everyone and everything with which we are interacting in that moment.

The energy we exchange travels within the null zones that are inherently within us and communicates with our particulates. When our particulates receive this new information they rearrange, creating a new environment or reality within us.

It is not simply the words that we exchange with other people that make a difference; it is also the subtle energies that accompany those words. What we are feeling, experiencing, even sensing, becomes transferred along with the communication that we are making (see Figure 15).

Figure 15: We Are Made of Energy

We are made of the same particulates of which the rest of entirety is created. When we interact with others, the energy we are expending is transferring to them via the null zones. At the same time, you are receiving communications and energy from others through the null zones.

If we are in a higher state of consciousness, the energy that we transmit to others moves through them more easily and communicates more fully because the energy is of a higher frequency. The energy contains more light.

When we are in a higher state of consciousness, we are able to make immediate differences with our every thought, movement or word.

Our emotional states have everything to do with how our energy is projected and how our energy affects others. When we are in a state of unconditional love, when we have accessed the union of our consciousness and our body, our energy travels smoothly, lightly.

When, for instance we are angry, our energy travels to others more as a blast which barrels through the null zones, all the while communicating not only the thoughts or words, but the energy of the emotion as well. It is in this way that moods are contagious. When people are laughing, joyful, we cannot help but begin to feel joyful too. When people are "downers" to us, it is because they are transmitting their feelings with their energies (see Figure 16).

When we exchange energies with others and we give or receive energies that are uncomfortable within us, such as those of anger or other negative feeling emotions, we have a tendency to attempt to protect ourselves from those energies. Unfortunately, once those energies are within our construct and we try to protect ourselves from them, what we end up doing is actually closing those energies within our own energetic fields in which the energies ultimately condense and become blockages in our energetic bodies (see Figure 17).

All the while energy is being exchanged between people, it is also being emitted into the environment. That energy leaves residual effects because it has entered into the null zones within the environment just as it did within the bodies and has communicated what we have sent or received outwardly into the Universal process. This is why some places feel quite good when we visit them while other places feel forbidding and negative. An imprint has been left there due to the exchanges of energy during, perhaps, an event or other interactions among people.

Figure 16: Energy Exchanges

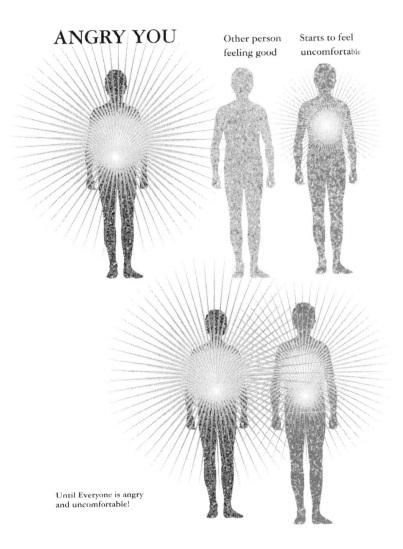

Figure 17: Examples of Blocked Energy

When our energy pathways are blocked we may feel sluggish or experience illness or pain.

We are at all times creating aspects in the Universal process that change what the Universe communicates to all other aspects of itself. We begin to realize that we are not individuals with only a personal stake in our existence. On the contrary, we truly are a part of all things, and all things are a part of us!

At the same time that we are experiencing sending and receiving, we are doing something else that is equally if not even more important.

We are holding a place of balance within the construct of the universe! Our particulates and null zones, although manifested as us, continue to be a unique part of the universal construct with a harmonic resonance that is the only one of its kind. Our harmonic resonance is a part of the totality of universal harmonics which holds actual space within the construct.

We are an interactive part of the living universe.

Since we serve as an integral part of the whole, it becomes easy to see why we serve our purpose each and every moment of our existence.

Our purpose is much larger than any single event. It is contributive to the interactive communication on every plane of existence.

Chapter Six
On Soul Entry and Death

Incoming

One of the most frequently asked questions in all belief systems is: when does a soul actually enter the body? At conception? Sometime during the pregnancy? At the moment of physical birth? When?

I had the privilege to bear witness to this process during a healing session that I was performing with a young woman. The young woman came to me as a part of a family unit who were seeking counseling assistance for relationship issues and the spiritual aspect of their lives in general. This particular young woman was quite open to Metaphysical and spiritual work and eager for change to take place in her life. As a result of her openness, I was able to see and access more levels than I generally do in a first or even second session.

I began the session in the usual way, establishing basic balance of the energy systems near her body. This allows for me to move into an easier state of visibility of the more etheric aspects of my clients. As I returned to the young woman's head area to begin the next phase of the session, there standing at her crown was a most beautiful creature.

This being was radiant, a light body which emitted silver blue light that moved in sweeping waves as he moved. He was touching my client lovingly and looking at her with pure heart in his eyes. He was emanating love from every aspect of his being. At first I thought this being might be one of my client's guides — as I see them often — yet something was different. How he felt, the way he looked at her... the Light that came from him. So I asked who he was...And... Oh... of... course... to my surprise he was a soul being!

At once I was filled with the knowledge that this soul being had arrived to become the young woman's child and was awaiting the moment of entry. It seemed that this beautiful being was waiting for permission to come into this woman's life and, further, for a certain event to occur so that he could make his entry.

I have to admit to being at a bit of a loss in that moment. Knowing what I was witnessing was overwhelming *me* to say the least! I was practically on my knees with emotion. This was sincerely one of the most loving moments I had ever shared in any dimension. A soul waiting to become of our dimension, embarking on a new series of experiences and I was witnessing this!

Without telling the young woman what I was seeing, I asked her if she was pregnant and she answered "no". I asked her how she felt about having a family, and she said that she would be thrilled when that happened because her first pregnancy had resulted in a miscarriage.

Through the session I wondered what I should or should not reveal. I was attempting to fully comprehend what I was witnessing, and it was difficult to keep my mind quiet as I had so many questions of my own. I decided to have a conversation with this soul being in the way that I had spoken so many times with the Masters, telepathically.

As I continued to work with the young woman, I silently asked the soul being to show me the process of exactly how he would enter when the moment came. I also asked him to explain to me when and how the time would be right, and how he would know. The being showed me that at the point of conception — the moment that the ova and the sperm joined — there would be a singular release of energy which is extremely high in vibrational frequency and unlike any other type of energy release in creation.

Energetically, this release acts like an opening door, a reaching out, an invitation to the soul awaiting entry to cross the threshold from one plane of reality and into this one. A specialized energetic environment is created which allows the soul being to enter. In the moment of conception when the energetic door is opened, the soul being also opens energetically, harmonizing his frequencies to those within the opportunity which has been created. In essence, the soul being changes its frequency to the exact harmonic conditions which are present in the joining of the sperm and the ova.

Since it has perfectly harmonized to the conditions of the fertilization, the soul's essence infiltrates the dividing cells, *becoming a part of the consciousness* of the cells which begin rapidly dividing to become a human child. Since consciousness is pure energy, as those cells continue to divide, the consciousness of the entering soul being grows within the consciousness of all of the cells of the body.

The soul being showed me that once he entered the biological format, he would remember for some time who he was and from where he had come. He showed me that only after birth would the memories of his previous experiences begin to fade as he, then the new child, would be inundated with communications from his parents and everyone around him. He would be more dense, having manifested as a human child and would not be as easily receptive to the memories of his essence. He would be instilled with the reality to which he had come. I was fascinated.

Interestingly, the soul being who presented himself to me during the session with the young woman was in male form. In our telepathic conversation, as he was explaining the entry process to me, he told me that he would be experiencing this new life as a female child. What wonderful validation that we do experience lives as both male and female beings!

I have to confess that I really wrestled about just how much I would say to my client. After all, she had recently experienced the loss of her first pregnancy. I did not want to play her emotions in the event that something would change and the pregnancy did not occur. This was all new territory for me.

My client had no idea that I was having this conversation with her future daughter. I knew that she was open to Metaphysical concepts. Yet, how far could her reality go? How far did my responsibility go?

I decided to continue the conversation I had started with her by telling her that if in fact she felt ready to begin her family that there was a soul ready to come in. That all she needed to do was give her permission and it would be so. I have to say that this delightful young woman's feet barely touched the ground on the way out of my house that day. She couldn't wait to tell her husband.

Apparently they wasted no time inviting the awaiting being into their lives. Exactly nine months later my client had a beautiful baby girl. I wonder if the little one would remember me?

(A few months after this session, my grandson was born. On the way home from the hospital my son and daughter–in–law dropped by so I could spend some quality time with them and the baby. He was almost two days old. Recalling what the soul being had told me about remembering his journey for a short time, I leaned over to my beautiful new grandson and whispered to the soul being inside "do you remember?" He looked me square in the eyes and smiled!)

Past Life Patterns and Cellular Memory

As described in the above section, the soul essence enters the energetic field which opened at the moment of conception. Further, the essence remains a part of the consciousness of each dividing cell. As the cells continue to multiply, the soul essence continues to be within each and every cell of the growing human being.

The soul essence is literally energetically filling the growing baby with all of its memories and experiences since the Beginning. The consciousness of the newly forming baby is infused throughout the body of that child.

The cells of the new child retain a memory of the soul being's consciousness and all that the soul being's consciousness has experienced from the Beginning. The memories of all time are infused within the entirety of that new child!

Of course, this gives the term "going within" a whole new perspective! We are literally created of our own essence and the essence of all of our soul's collective experiences all the way back to the Beginning!

Twins

In maternal, or identical twins, there are two soul beings who have come forward to become the new children. At conception, the two souls enter in the same moment, infiltrating the dividing cells with the essence of both consciousnesses.

One egg has been fertilized but divides into two separate parts which will ultimately become two children who look and seem identical. As the cells begin to divide into two completely separate and different children, each child carries certain aspects of the consciousness of the other.

Since the cells which ultimately divided to create the two separate children experienced a few moments of shared consciousness that shared consciousness remains as a minor, secondary aspect within the consciousness of each child. It is in this way that identical twins show amazing similarities in their lives and often exhibit telepathic abilities. It explains how these twins often experience parallel lives, even if they do not know each other, as, for instance, in the cases of adoption.

In the case of fraternal twins, two separate eggs are fertilized and two separate consciousnesses enter those eggs. There is no shared consciousness but often a mirroring of aspects as the two consciousnesses are so closely linked during the formation of the children. These twins may experience many similarities, but not to the extent that identical twins do.

Transplants and Affectations

As we move throughout our lives our consciousness collects and remembers all of our experiences. Those memories are retained within not only our etheric aspects but our physical bodies, our tissues and organs, as well.

There have been stories of situations in which transplant recipients began to have certain memories pertaining to the life of the organ donor. There have also been events when the transplant recipient actually began to crave foods that were the donor's favorite or even display attributes of the donor's personality.

This is because the recipient of the organs now has within them, within their tissues, certain aspects of the consciousness of the donor.

Entry of the consciousness which is a fundamental part of the donated organ is not *usually* perceivable on a cognizant level; nevertheless, it is there. In fact, the presence of the new aspect of consciousness may never be forefront in any way as the inherent consciousness of the organ recipient will generally outweigh the presence which accompanied the new organ.

There are times, however, when consciousness that has entered the system via a donated organ may manifest exhibitions of certain changes in the desires, personality or behavioral attributes of the person who received the donated organ.

This situation also applies to blood transfusions. In this case, the consciousness of the donor does not remain resident indefinitely because the donated blood is utilized by the recipient's body and ultimately replaced as new blood cells replace those of the donor's. An organ is a more permanent structure.

Death is a Transition

Death: Beginning or End? When does the soul or spirit leave the body? What really happens? Is there really something out there in addition to this reality? Or is this all there is... the end... one life?

Once again I have been astounded by a moment of privilege as I was shown the answers to these questions and more. A good friend and client of mine called me from out of state one afternoon and said that her aged father had fallen and broken his neck. He was in intensive care and there were other injuries as well.

My friend knew in her heart that her father was planning to make his transition and she was calling me to ask if there was anything that I could do to assist him in his situation.

My friend asked me to take a "look" at her father and do what I could to help him. I told her that I was probably not supposed to fix him, but that perhaps I could to boost his comfort level and give him the strength to make whatever choice he needed in his journey.

I hung up the phone and began to work long distance on my friend's father. This began as a fairly routine session as I balanced the basics of the multi-level energetic systems.

As I worked, the norm shifted. While I began to work on the major energetic centers (which include the Chakras), the most amazing things began to happen.

In their healthy and most functional form, the Chakras are actually pyramidal in shape. (They do carry polarities, or a spin, and that spin is the spiral within the pyramid... they are not flat entities as is the general interpretation.) When the Masters and I make corrections to these energy fields, as they become balanced, charged or changed, they present to me in the form of small holographic pyramids, each having a specific color, or shade of the same color, which corresponds to the frequencies of the energy center on which I am working.

A perfect harmonization of all the energy centers presents to me as a perfect alignment of a row of holographic pyramids with each appearing in the appropriate color just above the corresponding energy field. When the pyramids are aligned to perfection, the harmonization creates an energy field over and around the person with whom I am working. That field, when established, is also holographic and pyramidal in shape.

Beginning above the crown area, I began to establish normal functioning of that energy center. As soon as this area was normalized, the color corrected and the pyramid suddenly began to emit a golden glow from the top as if someone had put on a golden capstone. I actually jumped because the apex of the pyramid lit up so quickly and so brightly. I had never seen this in relation to a person.

From above the crown, I moved in the order I generally follow in this part of the healing process. Each time an area perfected, the pyramid would appear in the appropriate holographic living color. Different from any of my previous experiences, as the pyramids formed, the apex, the entire top third of each pyramid, lit up with a radiating golden glow. Each pyramid was demonstrating a capstone!

After the second and then the third pyramid lit up I knew something major was happening. Something that, once again, I had never seen. I knew I was witnessing something fantastic, yet I didn't want my brain convincing me that it was something it wasn't.

Whenever new situations occur in my work, I ask for clarification or more information so that I can gain an understanding of what I am seeing. I am generally given full knowledge of the process to which I am being introduced as a kind of an energetic download that is full of information. I began to send questions out into the Universe and, as I questioned, I kept myself free of expectations and continued working while I waited for the answers to come in.

As I approached the mid-section of the body, the answers began to come. I was shown that all of the energy centers would light just the same as the ones I had already worked on. And they did. One after the other, the little holographic pyramids became the appropriate color in harmonic relation to the area on which I was working. Not only did they light, but they aligned perfectly, following the exact center of the body. The golden light in combination with the colors of the energy centers was almost too much even for my etheric eyes.

I was told that I was giving this man the balance and the energy to complete his "dying" process. Whew. And I had to call my friend back and tell her this? Well, okay. I always do what I am given. It is just that sometimes it isn't easy, even when people have asked!

I asked to be shown just what the dying process looked like from this point. Immediately I saw all of the major energetic centers lit and aligned as I described above.

There is a field of energy around each human being which looks very much like a cocoon. This is not the same as the aura — in fact, it is much larger. This is an energetic field which acts as a buffer and interpreter between our humanness and us as Universal beings. It is an interpretive field which steps down the higher frequencies to translatable data for us. In the same vein, this field also translates what we are sending out into harmonic frequencies that the Universe can understand.

As I watched, the energy field around this man also began to glow as a golden light. Just above the man's heart area, the field began to open in a perfectly straight line. It was opening slowly yet deliberately with what appeared to be surgical precision (see Figure 18).

I was then shown that the light body, soul body...the essence of this man (whatever name you wish to give), would exit through the new opening as the gap gradually but quickly became larger.

As he exited, he was pure energy. He poured upward, moving back and forth in a kind of an "S" motion as if he were literally wriggling out of his body. He still appeared to have some form. At least he seemed to have a recognizable shape similar to what he looked like while he was still in his body. I was seeing his essence, that part of the man which was pure consciousness, a traveling soul body that had finished yet another experience.

As the light body cleared out of the physical body, it began to dissipate. The energetic form that the essence of this man had had was coming apart, changing into a wisp of being-ness as he faded away.

The further the essence moved from the physical body, the more it began to dematerialize and slowly began to blend with the energies of the light toward which it was moving. My friend's father was experiencing his return back to the Source. He was going Home.

Figure 18: Death is a Transition

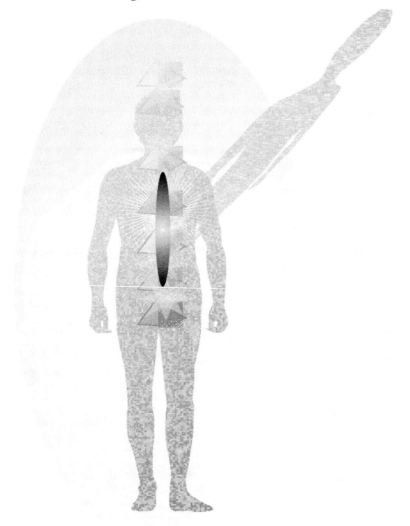

As the "dying" process begins, all of the Chakras begin to emit a golden glow, as if the have been installed with a radiant capstone. Then, the protective field around the body splits open and the essence of the person, or "soul" exits, leaving the corporeal body behind.

When I talked with my friend later on, I found out that in fact her father had transitioned shortly after our session.

Since that experience I have witnessed many variations of this transitional process. Soul beings, once free of the denseness of the corporeal body, may go through a variety of processes.

Soul beings that have completed their journeys, satisfied that they have successfully experienced all for which they have come, return directly to the Source, the Light. This is a direct process with no interruptions or stops along the way. They may be accompanied by other beings who they may or may not have known in the current lifetime.

Some soul beings make stops along the way back to the Source at various stages of vibrational frequency. I am told that these stages are for assimilating what has been learned in the life just past as well as a sort of re-attunement to the high frequencies of the Light.

This process varies in "time". As we have discussed in earlier chapters, all information is ultimately contained as light in energetic form in different sets of harmonic frequencies. Each soul being, or person, has a unique set of information based upon his or her experiences. That information has been stored within his or her essence and vibrational state of light being. Depending upon those experiences and at what vibrational rate the being was functioning during the time of transition, it may be necessary for that being to acclimate back toward the Source by stopping in stages to re-harmonize the light body as the frequencies become higher and higher.

These stops are very much like what an underwater diver does as he swims toward the surface of the water from a deep dive. Every 60 feet or so, he must stop and let his body equalize to the pressures surrounding him in the water. A soul who is moving toward the Light is moving out of a dense physical body as well as away from energies which are slower and heavier in the third dimension. These energies are very lethargic compared to what is experienced closer and closer to the Source. At times it takes some adjustment to re-harmonize to the higher frequencies.

Once the re-attunement has completed, the soul body becomes one with the Light in the same way that it was in the Beginning. There remain no actual memories of events, but a clear recognition of other beings. There is a sense of ecstasy, of being completely infiltrated with love. That *it is love*. Pure unadulterated bliss. At the same time, there is a connectedness to every thing and all things. A massive awareness that is conscious of all aspects of the Universal process at once. Not a thinking kind of a connection. A *knowing* connection. *Being* the One.

There are some soul beings that have a sense that things are unfinished, or who refuse to complete their transition until a loved one (such as a husband or wife) can travel with them. That bond which was forged in their relationship transcends time and space. When the remaining human person begins the transition process, the one who had departed earlier will come to meet him or her. Generally speaking, in these cases, these pairs of soul beings originated from the same aspects of Light in the earlier process of the Universal Manifestation. Often they are mirror images to each other harmonically. In these cases as the two come together, there is truly a sense of wholeness in a way that is not explainable in words, as if two halves have come together forming a whole. These are true twin flames. Soul mates.

Some departed soul beings remain at various dimensional levels to watch over certain members of the family or others to whom there is a strong tie. There can be more than one reason for this. There may be a sense of incompletion on the part of the departed, something left unsaid or undone, or one or more of those remaining on the earthly plane are keeping the departed soul from going any further in its journey.

Occasionally, those who have remained behind on the earthly plane actually hold the exiting soul close to this plane through their grief or inability to accept the reality of the "death" of the one who has departed. In a sense, they are creating a huge energetic vacuum out toward the departing soul being which can slow or even stop the soul's progress.

It can be quite difficult if not impossible for a departing being to "pull away" from those kinds of energies. In the same vein, when family members or loved ones are holding on so tightly, not accepting the departure of a loved one, it is often difficult for the soul essence of that loved one to leave the physical body and therefore there is the potential to actually *prolong* the "dying" process.

Soul essences often sense when they remain "stuck" at levels closer to the third dimension whether it is from a sense of incompletion or being held close by others. It really depends upon how far in their journey they were able to go before the soul essence became slowed or stopped. Soul beings that remain "stuck" in their travels may or may not manifest in this reality as "ghosts" or "spirits".

The transition of "death" or "dying" is not one to be feared. It is a celebration of achievement for each one who departs; for when one does, he or she is heading back toward that Source from which we have all originated.

Becoming a part of the Light again is the "home" that pulls at all of us from within. Death is nothing more than a transition of our existence from one aspect of being-ness to another. To resist that which we have come to do is to delay the very lessons our souls came to learn.

Near Death Experiences

As the transitioning soul begins its journey out of the physical body, the soul essence passes through the protective field that has opened in the moment of transition. While the essence begins its journey out of the body and heads for the opening of that field, the consciousness of the transitioning person has begun to lose perception of the energetic field of the physical body.

The energetic field, in a sense, created a perception of light for the consciousness as long as the consciousness was a part of that energetic environment. It also contained within it the sense of bodily inhabitation. As the consciousness travels from the physical body outward toward the opening of the field, there is a perception of darkness that resembles a dark tunnel. Through the opening in the departing field of energy, there is the perception of a bright light as the consciousness moves back toward its Source.

The energy field of a human being acts much like a veil between the realities of the third dimension and other planes of reality. As this field opens for the transition, and the essence of the person who is transitioning begins to exit that field, the veil is no longer a barrier to higher realities. Once the consciousness begins to leave the protective field, his or her harmonic signature enters other planes unhindered. Others who have transitioned previously recognize that signature frequency and gather to welcome the departing soul home.

Upon leaving the body there is a sense of great love as the essence, the consciousness becomes free of the encumbrances of the physical body and begins to experience the oneness that is inherent in the universal process.

If it is truly time for the essence of the transitioning person to leave the body and return to the Source, there will be a complete separation from the physical manifestation. If there are reasons for staying in the third-dimensional life, or if there are others still remaining in the third-dimensional reality that are energetically pulling at the transitioning person to stay, the essence of the transitioning person will then return to the physical body with a memory of a "near death experience".

Chapter Seven
The Akashic Records

When we learn to use our consciousness aside from our physical selves as an energy form which is unbounded, we begin to access our finer aspects, our ethereal selves. As we do this, we begin to operate from within our Light bodies, our true essence. Since our Light bodies are created of the same particulates and null zones of which all other things are made, they know how to move about the Universal process freely, communicating in the most basic ways with all other particulates.

As we learn to function in this way and we begin to explore the Universal processes with our consciousness, we begin to operate within the Universal mind, or consciousness. As our consciousness moves through the corridors of the null zones, we begin to understand complicated information completely and in a very simple fashion.

The information that we exchange with other particulates along the way becomes a part of us. Remember, all of the information within the fabric of the Universe is retained in light form, which means all of the information that is and has ever been is accessible to our conscious self in the same form that our conscious self exists. As energy. As Light. This information is often referred to as the Akashic records.

The Akashic records are not kept in a room somewhere out in the Universe; rather, they are held within the fabric of the Universal construct in the same form of light that comprises all of the particulates.

These records are contained within the Universal consciousness.

This means that because we are made of these same particulates, the same light, we carry within us all the information that ever was and is. We are a walking library. Further, since our consciousness is pure energy, it travels throughout the corridors of the null zones as a pure energy form which carries the communications of change throughout the Universe.

In and of ourselves, we are all of the information and the access to that information which we seek.

Information remains in Light form, growing in every moment as everyone and everything in the Universal process is continually experiencing, emitting and expending energy. As we discussed in Chapter One, all of the energy that is used and created is ultimately Light. Each time there is even the slightest emission or consumption of energy, the Universe changes. The Universe is never, ever, the same from one moment to the next.

By accessing the Akashic Records, the information that is held within our consciousness awakens to our command. The information that we have sought awakens within us. Because that information has become a part of our consciousness, our very being, we understand that information fully and usually immediately.

Once we have learned to access the Akashic Records as conscious energy, we can visit any place, event, person or time. When we travel in this way, we become a participating observer. A participating observer remains in awareness of their current manifestation but is also able to experience other realities with full or partial sensory awareness of those new realities at the same time. In this type of experience we are actually acting as multi-dimensional beings.

Often when this is the case, the experiences that we gain from within the Akashic records is brought back to the cognitive forefront and may be remembered or utilized as a real experience. We may bring back to our local reality intricate details, perceptions and sensory experiences from whatever time or place we have visited.

What we learn "out there" is very real. Learning in this way, accessing knowledge from time immemorial is complete in content and detail. When we bring other-dimensional information back with us, we are often able to apply that information to most any situation in our earthly lives, often enhancing or enriching our journeys as we begin to view them from different perspectives.

We can find relationships between our past and current lives or those of our clients, which may bring resolution to certain Karmic situations, or at least an awareness of those longstanding patterns of behavior.

We can look into the future. We can visit other places, other planets, other dimensions. We are unlimited in the information that is at our disposal.

As always, travels from a perspective of pure consciousness require discernment. We must remain functional in our third-dimensional existence, so how often and for how long we remain "out there" must be taken into consideration. It is always our choice what we glean from these experiences and how we use the information.

Chapter Eight
Karma

What is Karma and why is it so important? Is it real? How do we carry situations from one lifetime to the next?

In Chapter Six when we learned about incoming souls, we discussed how, when a soul enters newly dividing and developing cells during the moment of conception, those cells are filled with the essence of the entering soul being. The soul being joined the new environment as pure energy, and that energy was ultimately created of Light. We have already learned that Light carries information and memories.

The soul being introduced to the growing life a unique harmonic signature, a signature that the soul being has carried throughout all of its lifetimes. A soul being also brings in all of the information and memories that it has accumulated throughout its experience — not to mention all the memories of the Universe from the Beginning.

The entire body of the new life is filled with all of the information that was brought by the soul essence. Part of that information is about unresolved feelings or situations that the soul has carried from one life to the next. It becomes an inborn desire of the new child to bring resolution to those things that are unfinished from previous lives and to change other aspects of its soul journey in the new lifetime.

During the process of the new child's life span — as the child grows and matures — situations which provide an opportunity to resolve unfinished situations will be drawn to the child from deep within its essence. In other words, information which is retained in the form of energy throughout the child's being will communicate from its particulates into the Universal process, asking for the desired opportunities to create resolution of remaining situations.

When those communications move into the Universal process, realities are created which allow the soul being in its new lifetime opportunities to create those changes.

Often the process of resolution is accomplished by recreating situations or the dynamics of certain types of situations that occurred in other lifetimes so that the situations may be experienced in a different way, or so that different choices can be made that will change the path of the soul's journey altogether.

When, during a lifetime, certain types of situations continually repeat themselves, it generally means that the person who is experiencing those situations is making the same choices over and over again, or that he or she is reacting to those situations in the same way or a very similar way each time. To avoid repetition of situations, one simply must choose a different resolution or reaction to the problem. As soon as a different choice is made, the Karmic issue is completed and the pattern of repetition is broken.

For example, when a Karmic situation presents to a person, that person might exhibit a reflexive response by reacting to the situation from fear of that situation becoming like past situations that were painful or uncomfortable in some way. By reacting in this reflexive way, the person has actually made the situation not only worse, but has perpetuated the Karmic chain by allowing themselves to repeat a familiar pattern. The end result becomes all that the person feared in the beginning. If, when that person is presented with a situation that is fearfully familiar, a different choice is made, that new choice will not only change how the situation develops, if it develops at all. That new choice will forever break the Karmic pattern.

We can create Karma as well. By our actions, thoughts and words, all of which are energy, we put out into the universal process those things that we are communicating with others and ourselves. As we do, we are calling to the universe to bring us exactly what we have created.

For instance, when we call upon the infinite for the healing of others, we are also calling for healing of ourselves. When we wish for peace in other places, we ultimately find peace within ourselves. This works negatively as well. When we wish harm or bad will toward others, we are also asking for that to be brought to us. After all, are we not a part of the whole? That which we create becomes our reality.

Karma is literally a cause and effect situation. That which we cause affects us. This is a universal law. All things within the universal construct react from cause. Energy travels through the null zones, communicating with the particulates, and the particulates reorder to create a new reality on some level. When we communicate into the universal process, we are sending energy through the null zones which is communicating with the particulates "out there" to create a new reality. We must be careful of what we set out that may come back to haunt us!

Often souls who have had previous lifetimes together will meet again in a new lifetime to complete or change situations which have remained between them. One soul may become a catalyst for another to grow. Another may come to demonstrate validation or a loving relationship to another. There are countless reasons that souls come together to share experiences in a given lifetime. Again, as long as different choices are made, patterns are broken and the Karma becomes completed.

In many cases, such as romantic relationships or friendships, people have come together to satisfy Karmic situations. Once the Karmic conditions have been filled, the people who have come together have satisfied their reason for being together. When that is the case, those people often go separate ways. As human beings, this is often hard to understand because emotional aspects are also at play, causing people to hang on together for reasons that make no sense in the whole picture. This often causes hurt feelings or feelings of abandonment or rejection when, simply put, the relationship has served its purpose and it is time to move on.

One of the ways that Karmic issues present to me in healing sessions is when I access the soul body, the very essence of the client, the soul body may be surrounded by old books or scrolls. Each of these books or scrolls represents a Karmic situation. Those that are completed will appear golden and locked closed, while others that are still in progress appear to be unused or creating clutter around the soul body. Some people have very little Karmic resolution to finish, while others appear to have collected nearly very situation they have ever encountered without finishing those situations!

Some Karma that is collected during the journey of the soul does not need to be finished. This is because during one lifetime or another, the soul has chosen a different path that no longer includes those lessons or situations. These manifest to me during sessions with others as some of the clutter I mentioned earlier. Even though those situations are no longer necessary, they still leave energetic clutter that must be cleared. Once cleared, the person is able to perceive and make choices to resolve or change remaining Karma much more clearly.

The journey of the soul is a complex and multi-faceted experience. Any one choice which is made can change the entirety of not only the path of the human being, but the remaining needs for fulfillment or growth during the journey of that soul being.

One of the questions we are most often asked is if people have completed all of their Karma. My observation is that many of those asking this question do not want to be active and conscious parts of their journey, rather, just have it all magically done for them. Nothing can ever be complete in our passage unless we play an active part in our own process. The answer to this question is quite simple:

If one has completed all of the Karma that is created for the growth of that being, then that being has no further need to journey as a corporeal being unless it is by the choice of that soul to return as a Master who has come to teach others about the meaning of perfection.

As we move into the photon belt, we are being inundated by Light particles. Since all of the Karmic information is stored as energy in our bodies and energy is ultimately Light, the influx of photon particles may actually assist us in resolving karmic issues.

Our entire beings are becoming more responsive from the Light within us and into our daily experiences. The vibrational rates of our very beings are rising in frequency, and it is easier to access more of our issues in this lifetime. This is because as our vibrational rates increase, we become closer to Light and therefore have more access to information which is stored as Light.

The higher the vibrational rate, the closer to Light we are.

Our particulates respond to the photon energy and the higher frequencies by separating in mathematical increments. The size of the increments of separation as well as the direction of separation depends upon the rate of incoming frequencies such as those we are receiving from the photon particles, and the length of stimulation by those frequencies.

As the particulates move into those incremental separations, in some cases, they become more exposed, more accessible. Because the particulates are more accessible, our consciousness has more opportunity to bring forward the information that has been stored there throughout our lifetimes. Once brought to the surface, Karmic issues may easily be recognized, addressed, completed and released.

It is quite possible, even probable, because of the existing energetic levels, that during our current lifetimes we may be able to experience and release many of the Karmic situations which we have carried for eons. I call this "Karmic Fast Forward".

It is always our choice, once confronted with circumstances, whether to remain in familiar situations or to step outside of those situations and into a different avenue of being.

It is not necessarily important to remember the details of past lives or situations that may have become Karmic for us. The details aren't all that important. What is important is to recognize the repetitive patterns which occur throughout our lives, particularly the ones that come up time after time or that make us feel bad. As we begin to distinguish these patterns, we become able to create change in our experiences.

Once we have begun to create positive changes in our existence, releasing old patterns literally from within our beings, we become free of past situations forever and our experiences become completely different than we had known before.

Chapter Nine
Dimensional Shifts

Next to the word "energy", one of the most overused words in Metaphysics is "shift". Shifts are referred to as changes in consciousness, planetary alignments – such as the polarity of a planet on its axis – and more often as a dimensional change in alignment.

A dimensional shift occurs when there is a massive change in the balance of the consciousness within that dimension. This can occur by extreme growth of either the consciousness of the Light or the Dark energies.

Remember, dimensions are formed in the same manner and pattern as the particulates. They are octahedrons which are aligned inwardly and outwardly from one dimension to the next. All of the dimensions have empty spaces in between which are just larger variants of the null zones.

Typically, when a dimensional shift occurs, the entire octahedron changes its alignment with the surrounding dimensions. Literally, the dimension rolls into a new position within its space, thus creating new harmonic relationships within itself and all other dimensions. This may cause a shift in the reality within the dimension as well.

When shifting of dimensional alignment is created from a higher balance of Light, the reality changes to one of a higher nature. That reality may resemble Utopian descriptions, or those of Nirvana, because within the new harmonic relationships there are higher vibrational frequencies and therefore more Light.

Those negativities which had plagued the dimension prior to its change of alignment are no longer present or effective.

In situations when Darkness has ruled the balance of forces, there is an opposite effect. Negativities rule and that of the Light is all but forgotten. At the time of a shift resulting from Darkness, negativities outweigh other positive natures. What once was a viable and pleasant place to live becomes a place of darkness, death, destruction and illusion.

The direction and timing of a dimensional shift are absolutely related to the consciousness of those who reside within that dimension.

In other words, the consciousness of everyone in that dimension is directly responsible for the balance within that dimension, or ultimately a shift of that balance.

It is possible within a unification of consciousness toward a singular purpose to effect a change in the balance of energies within a dimension.

The consciousness of each being within the dimensional realm contains a unique base frequency that is a part of the established norm of harmonics within that dimension's organization of frequencies. As each person within a group projects an intended reality or realities into the universal process, the individual signature frequency of each person (therefore harmonizing as a group) is projected with that new intended reality. In this way, there is a new harmonic relationship developed which may ultimately cause the dimension to shift its positional relationship causing new relationships with other surrounding dimensions.

Once critical mass, or full harmonization of consciousness toward a specific purpose, is reached, the dimension shifts toward the projected reality. The newly created reality becomes that which was consciously projected.

In this way, entire worlds and relationships within those worlds can be changed. Unfortunately, a dimensional shift within the third dimension is a rarity since human nature is one of individuality and diversity, and unified consciousness is almost never achieved.

But it *is* possible.

Section Three

The Healing

Of the One

Chapter Ten
Being a Healer

While this chapter is about what it takes to be a good etheric healer, it is also about how we must exist within ourselves and our lives in general when we work within the universal construct. Who we are, who we believe we are, and what we believe has everything to do with the outcome of our Seventh Sense™ journeys.

When we make demands of the universal process to create new realities, our energy and our essence go outward into the very processes from which we create those new realities. The principles which are addressed in this and the following chapters may be applied to anyone who chooses to work within the Seventh Sense™ and beyond.

In the next few chapters I use the term "healer" broadly because when we work within the One, creating new and higher realities for ourselves, our world and others, are we not working as healers of the One?

When we begin to view our realities from the standpoint of our Seventh Sense™, we realize that there is much more to us than simply our physical bodies. We begin to see that we are comprised of many localized layers and otherdimensional levels of energy fields as well as multiple energy bodies, each serving us in a different way. Healers who specialize in alternative methods have already begun to discover how to address and create changes to many of these energy fields and bodies.

There are a lot of aspects to being a good healer. Just wanting to help people isn't enough, although that is a good start! One must be of the highest integrity. A healer must first be able to be honest with him or herself, and then learn how to convey that honesty in constructive ways to others.

The healer must be centered and balanced from within and have no investment or expectations toward the outcome of any session.

One must allow the energies to flow to and for the client and, at the same time, provide the client a safety zone where he or she can experience a sense of freedom to accept the healing on all levels. One who does healing work must never, ever, approach the healing of another person with anything but loving positive feelings. If there are personal issues to be dealt with on the part of the healer, those issues must be resolved prior to working on anyone.

Ego has no place in the healing forum. It is not what we can do, but what we allow to be done through us.

Very importantly, if a healer doesn't have answers to the client's questions, the healer should be honest enough to say so. This can be done in several ways. The healer may simply say that the information hasn't been given, or that the information has not come in completely. It is okay to research information to get a fuller meaning for the client; in fact I encourage it.

For instance, in one long distance session I worked with a man who had been in the military and had been all over the world working in covert operations. He was extremely sick, having contracted some strange type of parasites during his travels. Apparently the military had given him treatments which had caused his illness to progress to near death. The entire time I worked, I kept getting the word "turpentine".

"God," I thought, "that is *poisonous*! Why would I tell this man something like that as a *remedy*?"

To make a long story short, I researched my findings before contacting the client, and lo and behold, *oil* of turpentine has been used for many years in the treatment of certain parasites! What a relief! I was then able to contact the appropriate professional for further information to pass on to the client with a caveat due to his condition. (Since I am not a medical doctor, I cannot prescribe cures, only give information that I am given during the sessions. The client may then choose whether or not to pursue the information further.)

When we do this type of healing work, there are many times when we truly don't understand what some of the bits and pieces of information mean. It is okay to say so, and further, it is just fine to admit that we need to find out more. Discretion is the key. Sometimes we get information which, if given to the client, would interfere with his or her journey.

As healers, we must weigh that information as to the benefit of the client. For instance, I worked with a woman who told me that a previous healer had said that this woman's husband was going to transition, to die (he wasn't even sick), and that she would find someone else to fulfill her life.

The woman immediately ceased interaction with her current husband and began having an affair with an old flame from years past on whom, as a school girl, she had had a large crush. He was also married. This went on for years. In essence, the woman stopped participating in her marriage because someone else told her that something would happen. True, the woman made her own choices, but would she have made those same choices if she had not been given that information? Years later, her husband is alive and well and quite confused at the state of his relationship with his wife and they are both miserable!

It comes down to being responsible for what is said and how it is stated! Sometimes the wisdom is in the silence.

All beings and particularly healers must remember that when energy is expended it must be replenished. In our society we are taught to give to others, but we are rarely taught to receive. This generally leads to awkwardness when others want to do things for us. It can also lead to feelings of unworthiness.

One must not give and give and not get back. After all, we must maintain our own energy levels if we are to assist others with theirs! We must allow ourselves to receive whatever we need in order to stay well and whole.

My friend Betty puts this beautifully: "Going with the flow means actually being *in the flow as a part of it*." In other words, it isn't about giving ourselves and our energy away; it is about being within that flow of energy so that we are constantly replenished as we work. This absolutely requires being present in the moment.

(When others attempt to help us, or give us something special, if we do not accept we deprive them of the gift of giving!)

A healer must understand and know in his or her heart that he or she is not responsible for the outcome of any session. When I first began my healing practice I felt responsible for the healing of everyone that came to see me. After all, *I was the healer*, right? No, not right at all! I soon learned that I am a vessel, an instrument for healing, but that I am not responsible for the outcome!

The energies that we work with are those of the universal process. Those energies are that of which all things are made. It is up to the client whether or not those energies are accepted for healing of any kind. The healer is only an instrument to be worked through for the direction of those energies.

What it comes down to is not necessarily what the healer did or did not accomplish, but rather how well the client accepted the healing.

Healing cannot be an ego-based event in any situation; however, extreme gratitude can certainly be expressed by the healer for having been a part of that healing process!

For a healer to be truly effective, that healer must have first healed him or her self. As we have seen in previous chapters, our energy passes from one to another in the course of interacting with each other. The same holds true for healers. The difference is that the process of sharing energy is amplified by the healer's intent and direction of those energies as well as the receptivity of the client.

When we as healers present ourselves to the public, offering our services, we must be certain that what we are offering is pure. If we are holding within us issues that are unresolved, such as anger, grief or other seemingly negative situations or emotions, we are at risk of transmitting those issues energetically to our clients or patients.

For example, years ago, when I was very new at experiencing alternative health methods, I began going to a specialized massage therapist. This healer also used energy along with her massage methods. Each time this therapist worked on me, I experienced a welling up in my body of severe anger. It would course through my body and up my arms. The angry energy that I felt was nearly intolerable and was so intense that I often felt as if I was coming out of my skin. The anger did not fit any part of my emotional memories or experience and was often accompanied by ancient visions of conflict. These feelings were very confusing to me, especially since I am generally quite direct and as a rule I don't carry those kinds of feelings past a situation!

When I asked the massage therapist why I experienced those feelings, she said that I was having "releases" and that this was normal. She indicated that those were feelings that I did not recognize. Her explanation did not ring true for me. I found out later that it *is* quite typical to experience emotional or other types of releases during certain types of body work. However, the emotions that I experienced during sessions with that therapist *really were not mine.* They were those of the therapist and they were *transferring to me!*

Being quite sensitive to others, as the therapist's energy flowed through me with her work, her emotional issues were moving through my body and I was experiencing them! *I was feeling anger that had been repressed by this therapist.* Further, the visions I had were of past life circumstances that also belonged to the therapist!

When I realized what was happening, I talked with the therapist, explaining what I understood. The therapist denied having any issues of anger and told me that the anger I felt was all *mine.* After several attempts to help not only myself, but this otherwise gifted healer, I realized that the situation was not resolvable at that time and I simply stopped going there. I never experienced those kinds of feelings again!

That experience was a valuable lesson to me in many ways. It was the opening of an entire new set of intuitive gifts that I didn't know I had. Secondly, several years later I began to offer my services as a healer. Much due to that experience and before I agreed to work with the public, I spent a great deal time in self examination emotionally, mentally, spiritually. I worked toward keeping my physical self in healthy condition as well. My goal was to share only positive healing with my clients!

In short, we must be cautious not only of our own issues, but selective about whom we allow to touch us in the name of healing. Of course, not everyone is so sensitive that they would experience the negative energies of others; nevertheless, the potential for adverse effects remains.

Finally, a healer must always be protected. What do I mean by this? When we step out into other realities, if we are not strong of heart, will and intent, and working from the purest of places within ourselves, we may be subject to taking on energies from our clients or entities that we would not care to have in our space. Those energies in the short run or over time can make us sick or give us feelings of imbalance. These situations may not be obvious to us until we become of greater experience.

The most excellent way to become protected is to *ask for protection* from whomever we wish, be it God, the Angels, our Guides ... whomever!

My personal method is to imagine that Light begins deep in my center of being, moving outward through my physical self and outward through and beyond all my etheric selves...basically that I AM the Light. In this way, I am *becoming* the Light of the Source and working *as* that Light and therefore will not take on undesirable energies or passengers!

Secondly, we must *believe* that we are protected and never, ever work in the etheric realms with any sense of fear at all. Remember in the manifestation chapter where like attracted like as the Light manifested into the pyramids, octahedrons, and finally, tangible matter? Similarly, our state of mind, heart and soul has everything to do with the kind of help and protection that we get "out there"!

Chapter Eleven
Being Well

Our bodies, our selves, are sacred spaces with many, many sets of harmonic arrangements that are comprised of particulates which have arranged in the manifestation as us. There is a fine balance in the normal arrangements of our particulates.

When we have dysfunctions in our energy fields or in our etheric bodies, those dysfunctions may ultimately reflect as discomfort or pain at our physical level. Healing with the Seventh Sense™ and other types of energy work address and adjust the harmonic relationships of the energy fields and bodies, directing them to change in actual form toward a healthier arrangement...but more about that later...

First of all, *we are responsible for our own healing. What we believe becomes our reality; therefore we must believe that we are already well.*

Sometimes, it takes the direction or skills of another person or persons to help us into a place of healing within ourselves. We must believe in that person's abilities as much as we believe in our own abilities to be well.

Our healing also depends upon our emotions, as many, many illnesses are caused by unprocessed or repressed emotions. To be well and stay well we must be willing to do our part toward that wellness. We must be open and honest with ourselves, cleansing ourselves of unwanted emotional baggage, letting go of past situations that do not serve us any more. Most of us come from backgrounds with at least some dysfunction or have carried some emotional baggage with us into adulthood.

Rather than defending painful situations to ourselves or others as excuses for our behaviors, we must learn to deal with those situations and then let them go. To do so requires a great deal of self honesty which most of us have avoided because it just hurts too badly. The main reason we carry old stuff around is because we didn't have the skills, the emotional tools, to work through those situations at the time they happened.

At the time we experienced many of the situations we carry with us throughout our lives, many of us took on responsibility for the actions of others. In the meantime those who "hurt" us have gone on with their lives never knowing how they affected us!

This does not mean that we did not have some part in the situation, but if we use that part as a springboard toward self understanding and growth we can move on into healthier spaces of awareness.

If we allow ourselves to process and release those old emotional issues we literally become much lighter within our energetic systems and they can flow more freely toward keeping us well.

We must heal ourselves spiritually. Many of us live in conflict as to what we actually do believe. It goes far beyond what we *believe* to what we allow ourselves to experience, to be, to *know*.

What we know inside – way deep down inside – is the Truth that resides within each of us. It really doesn't need a name, it just is. When we can connect with that part of ourselves that *is* Truth, we find that feeling that we all seek throughout our lives.

The feeling I am referring to incorporates a fullness that is immeasurable...the God Self that we all are. That place within us is a love so immense that no words can do it justice. Words are limiting; this feeling is infinite! When we operate from that very special place within ourselves, we do so from pure unconditional love and are available for whatever energies are needed toward the healing work we do.

When we find ourselves out of balance in some way and feel that we need help to get back on the healing path, we often seek the assistance of an experienced healer. When we request healing from another person, whether he or she is a medical professional or an Alternative Healer, we must also be willing to *accept* the healing we seek.

We must also be discerning about who we ask to assist us. Because of our makeup, the harmonization that ultimately became who we are, there are some people who feel disharmonic to us, who "rub us the wrong way". Even when we can see no conscious reason for this, it is sometimes simply a matter of others operating at different levels of vibrational functioning – different harmonic frequencies. The harmonic frequencies of their particulates are disharmonic with our own. This does not become a judgment question of good or bad, but simply a question of harmonic resonance between people. So it is best to find a healer who "feels" right!

Real healing isn't just an emotional band aid, it is serious business. Many people seek healer after healer and never seem to get well. It isn't that all of those healers weren't good at what they were doing; rather that those people who didn't become well may not have really *wanted* to be well. I call this comfortable discomfort. Sometimes it is easier to stay stuck in what we know than to move into a different state of being which is unfamiliar to us.

There are many reasons why people don't get well, even when they have asked for help. **Most actual healing is done purely by the acceptance of it by the client.** In other words, one must *really want* to be well on all levels, *accepting* the healing energies that come. If they do, and it is meant to be, healing will occur.

Sometimes no matter what a healer does, some people just don't find wellness.

It is possible that those people really need nurturing of a different kind – more attention at home or in life in general. Many people look to others to fill a sense of emptiness that can only be filled from within. In this case, a healing session is a temporary fix but doesn't solve the sense of lack in the client.

Another reason that people do not become well after one or more healing sessions is that they may have accepted the perception that they are not worthy to receive the healing or they may have the idea that they are imperfect. As long as a view of imperfection remains, complete healing is not likely.

Perhaps the client does not believe deep inside that the healer really can help. If there is no faith in the healer, there can be no healing.

If the affliction is of a Karmic nature, or it is time for a person to transition from this plane to another, we as healers will not be able to change the situation. We can, however, establish balance and healing that will assist the etheric bodies and other energy fields to align and therefore have the strength to make the coming transition more easily.

Case in point: A dear friend of mine asked me to come to her town and perform a healing session with one of her best friends. Her friend had had many battles with cancer, and, after having been in remission for a while, was fighting for her life as the cancer had returned and was ravaging her body.

When I arrived at the friend's home, I was impressed with this woman's vitality. We talked at length and intuitively I was able to give her some information that would help her comfort. I understood that this beautiful woman really wanted to live. Even in her disease-battered body which had wasted to a tiny shadow of her original self, her spirit remained vibrant and she spoke positively about her future. She also accepted that if it was truly her time to go, she would, but she was afraid.

As I gently proceeded through our healing session it was necessary to be extremely careful because she was in so much pain. My heart was wide open, as I wanted to give her everything that I could. As we worked together, I began to smell roses. I looked up, and there was a magnificent Angel standing on the other side of the table. The Light was blinding. The Angel smiled majestically and dropped red rose petals down the length of my client.

Through my tears, I told my client what was happening, and she asked me the Angel's name, which I gave to her. We all cried loving, compassionate tears as the Angel stayed throughout the session, flooding the room with the scent of rose petals.

With every part of my being I knew that I had not come to help my vibrant new friend to live, but rather to help her find some balance and to ease her fear of leaving this world. And so she did a few weeks later, gracefully and without fear, and the beauty of her spirit remains not only in my heart but in the hearts of many even now.

In the case of Karmic situations, illness may be part of the learning process of the person who is experiencing the difficulty. The journeys of our soul bodies can bring challenges to our lives. There is much to learn about living and even dying, and we do not always understand what those challenges are, or why we face them. Sometimes we can't fix them and that just has to be okay. In the meantime we can do our best toward relieving pain, aligning the etheric aspects and sharing our love and compassion with those who need us.

Karmic situations may also involve others who are connected with the ill person, such as family or other loved ones. When someone is very sick, family members, friends and anyone else who is involved with that person go through a lot of thoughts and feelings. Often they find themselves having to give in ways they never imagined or doing things they never thought they would. Karmic circumstances can touch a lot of people in a lot of ways!

No matter what the reasons are for our challenges, being well is a constant journey. Wellness is a challenge to us which often results in the growth of who we are on many levels. It requires us to remain within our essences as integral parts of the One each and every moment that we exist. If we are open to wellness and do our parts toward well being, our lives become much richer and many of the fears that we have carried from past experiences are no longer valid.

Chapter Twelve
Alchemy and Transmutation

What is etheric healing, really?

Etheric healing is a process of alchemy and transmutation in which the matter of particulates is intentionally rearranged toward a changed reality of well being.

What we intend, we can create, because when we send out that intention we are simply telling the universal construct that we command a change in reality!

We learned that the particulates are octahedron-shaped particles that are aligned in particular ways based upon the harmonic relationships within each particulate. We learned that there are corridors between the particulates that carry energy — our thoughts, our prayers, our intentions, and information about what is happening throughout the entire universal construct.

At any given time, each particulate is aware — yes, consciously aware — of what all other particulates everywhere are experiencing. The particulates respond to that information, brought by the traveling energies, by rearranging their order. This, in the truest sense of the word, is an alchemic process because when the particulates rearrange, that create a new and different reality!

When we enter our Gamma states via Movement to Spirit™, we become unlimited in our creative powers. So how does it work?

When we move into the Gamma state, and our brain becomes a unified field of energy as described in Chapter Four, something incredible happens — we jump out of time and space. We begin to work within the universal construct as a *conscious part* of that construct. Our consciousness is able to deliberately work outside our physical state, unhindered.

When we are in the Gamma state, using our Seventh Sense^{TM}, our consciousness is moving faster than the speed of light!

J. S. Bell devised Bell's theorem which basically states that all particles are somehow connected and the effects of events are immediate, instantaneous – that those particles are "superluminal", faster than the speed of light.

Consciousness moves faster than the speed of light and is therefore not usually subject to the limitations of physical or general scientific principles. As pure consciousness, we become superluminal! Our consciousness can be everywhere and nowhere simultaneously and the effects of what we do are immediate!

We become able to move unfettered into any time, place or circumstance we intend. Since everything within all creation is manifested of the same format – particulates, each formed of a different set of frequencies – reality simply becomes different arrangements of those harmonic frequencies. Reality exhibits as varying densities of expression of the relationships between the particulates in those arrangements.

When operating as pure consciousness, we become capable of creating an expression of miracles! We can be everywhere and nowhere simultaneously. And we become able to work as multi-faceted beings in many dimensions at once, capable of working on all aspects of our client at the same time! Of course, this takes practice... a lot of it!

When we work in the Gamma state, we sense with every particulate of our being. We absorb and transmit huge amounts of information instantaneously. Knowledge literally and instantly becomes a part of us. If it is within the limits of natural law, we become able to project that knowledge into the universal construct as demands for the particulates to rearrange within diseased areas of our bodies or those of others. Once the rearrangement has occurred, a new reality exists and healthfulness occurs.

This is intentional alchemy and has the potential for complete transmutation.

We as conscious beings and healers have the capability to effect changes not only within our clients, but our environments and our world, as well!

In Medieval times, alchemy was considered a process of turning other metals into gold – basically, a transmutation of one form of matter into another. In ancient Egypt, alchemy was used as well, but generally to turn gold into a white powder which they called *mfkzt* which was thought to bring about immortality as well as physical vitality.

The white powder was made in a secret process that included heating the gold to high temperatures. As the gold was heated, it transmuted into a white powder which was then baked into loaves of bread. Many ancient Egyptian tombs have been found to contain these loaves as food for the decedent in the afterlife.

Scientists today have begun to re-create this ancient process. What they have found is that when gold is repeatedly heated and cooled, the nuclei of the atoms of the gold enter into a "high spin" state; that is, they begin to move extremely fast. In the normal state there are generally two electrons involved with these atoms with one moving clockwise and the other moving counterclockwise around the nucleus of the atom.

In the high spin state, all of the electrons begin to move in the same direction. When this occurs, the electrons become controlled by the nucleus of the atom. When this process is perfectly correlated, the atoms turn to white light and can no longer hold the substance together. The result is a white powder.

What is amazing is that when the gold is heated in a pan of sorts in the laboratory, and the white powder begins to form, not only the powder, but the pan goes inter-dimensional! The actual optimum weight of the powder and the pan lessen, and become invisible! As much as 44% of the optimum weight of the pan and the gold, now in the form of white powder, disappear!

So where does it go? Simply put, it has turned to light and begun to exist on a different plane of reality. It has gone inter-dimensional. The atoms have become superluminal. They have been transmuted by alchemic process!

There are both physical and non-physical ways to perform alchemy and transmutation. A physical example is the white powder. It is a tangible process that may be documented and measured. When we bring forth healing from within the universal construct, we, as a disembodied consciousness, are working superluminally in pure light form. That is a non-physical expression of our creative powers. The powers of consciousness are certainly not yet measurable or tangible but are certainly verifiable from the results that occur!

When we operate from within our Seventh Sense™ we can directly affect the form and behavior of matter, thus bringing change in reality! Healing from this perspective creates the reality of wellness.

We, as pure consciousness, become able to travel along the corridors, the null zones, between the particulates, communicating with the particulates the entire way. As we do this, the particulates rearrange toward a new reality.

When applied to our healing practices, we can literally take our consciousness inside a human body to create change from a more literal viewpoint. We can take our consciousness anywhere in the etheric and physical anatomy that is necessary to create the desired changes.

One very powerful session I experienced was when I was working with a young woman who is the daughter of a close friend of mine. This young woman had a congenital heart condition that involved a malformation of her aortic valve. This was causing malfunction of the operation of the heart. She had serious symptoms that included being fine one minute and then, with no warning, passing out cold the next. The symptoms had worsened, and her physician had told the young woman that she needed open heart surgery. He also told her that she could not risk having children because the stress on her heart might kill her. As a result, the girl had made a suicide attempt the night before. Upon finding her daughter in such a state, after giving her daughter the medical attention that she needed, her mother called me with an S.O.S. and brought her daughter to me for some counseling and perhaps a healing session as well.

I had a long, forthright and heartfelt conversation with this girl before ever touching her toward healing. It was important to establish her true state, and to find out if she really wanted to be there with me, or if I needed to refer her to more immediate intervention therapy of some kind.

Since we knew each other, we had already established trust between us and the young woman shared her innermost feelings with me. It seemed that her entire life plans and dreams were centered on having a family. If she was unable to do so, she felt that she had lost her purpose and therefore her reason to live.

Together, we agreed to work on all the aspects that were involved: the physical, emotional and everything in between.

During the healing session, I experienced huge waves of passion toward the wholeness and wellness of this girl. Her emotional pain was nearly tangible and her physical state quite fragile. I wanted so much to help her, and she was so ready for changes.

At one point my reality changed completely. No longer was I standing in the room with my client. Rather, I found myself standing inside her body, looking up at her aortic heart valve from the inside of her aorta! I could see the malformation of the valve and consciously directed repairs to the area. With amazement I watched as the problem vanished, and before me was a healthy heart and valve! Wow. *Wow!*

When we were finished, I told the young woman that I felt her heart problem would no longer manifest itself. After I had witnessed the heart repairs, I was told that my client would have a normal life and that she would have a little boy in the not too distant future. I shared this information with her as well. Needless to say, she left with an entirely new outlook.

I had honestly forgotten about this session, as there had been many others since. About a year later, my young client went for more tests on her heart and her doctors were amazed that the defect was no longer detectable. I have to admit that as often as I see these wondrous changes happen, I am continually awed at the reality of it all.

It is amazing what can happen through us when we give ourselves up to the experience. Of course we must believe in the abolition of impossibilities as well as in the reality we intend to create...and so must those who ask for help! Anything is possible when we believe in it!

Chapter Thirteen
An Etheric Anatomy

We have discussed the manifestation of all creation. We know each day when we look in the mirror who we see, what we look like, and how our looks change over time. What we don't see in the mirror is all the other parts that make us whole.

We are much more than skin and muscle, feelings, thoughts and emotions. We are energy fields with etheric bodies, grid lines and so much more. In this chapter we will discover how very special we are by experiencing an overview of how we are manifested far beyond our physical makeup and into multi-dimensional realities.

When we enter into our Seventh Sense™, our multi-dimensional awareness, we become able to see other aspects of ourselves. This includes our etheric makeup. Our etheric makeup consists of many basic aspects as well as a multitude of very subtle ones.

Combined, all those aspects contribute to the experience we have as third dimensional beings. When we access all of these parts of ourselves and others through our Seventh Sense™, we can effect change which in turn creates change in this dimension.

Some of those changes can be quite blatant, such as the disappearance of pain or healing of physical problems, while other changes may move into this reality on a much more subtle basis, such as energy patterns involved with higher etheric bodies that have been restored to healthful functioning. No matter what kinds of changes are made, those transformations are very real and ultimately make a difference in the overall experience of the person who has received them.

To attempt to give all the information that is available would take volumes of work. I have chosen to represent herein a basic etheric anatomy. The illustrations within this chapter are my humble attempts to recreate what I see ethereally. In some cases I have oversimplified the graphics for readability.

There are no words for the beauty that can be experienced throughout the dimensions. The colors that are seen "out there" cannot possibly be reproduced within this realm. The light on some planes of reality is so bright that it may actually hurt the etheric eyes.

The intangibility of most of the etheric aspects disallows even a meager attempt at reproduction of a scale in form. Formlessness seems to have no barriers other-dimensionally. Instead, those aspects which I see give rise to the idea of immeasurable possibilities.

There are no defined lines past our dimension. No segregate spaces, only boundless energy which presents in form and formlessness.

As the Masters always say, "...it is impossible to quantify that which is immeasurable." That being said, we move on to a description of the basic etheric anatomy...

Our Energetic Cocoon

We are surrounded by an etheric field of energy that looks much like a cocoon (see Figure 19). This energy field acts as both a transmitter and receiver to us. It is different from what we recognize as our "aura", which is an interior energy field and only a part of this cocoon.

As a transmitter, this cocoon tells the universal construct what we are experiencing, feeling and thinking as well as what we are attempting to create. It a major part of our communication system as manifested beings within the One. The harmonization of our particulates as whole beings communicates through this field of energy. From within our energetic cocoon we emit energy that is sent out into the universal construct much in the way that we see in Figure 19. In this manner, we communicate our experiences to all other forms of creation.

As a receiver, this energy field translates for us all the information that we receive from the Universe. This translation works in such a way that we are often able to bring into our thoughts and words what we sense from the One, even when we don't consciously realize what we are doing.

This cocoon also acts as a protective force around the manifestation of us. In a way, it helps to hold together our personal particulates while we take the form of human beings. This field can also collect energies that we do not want and can later affect us as illnesses or other problems.

As we interact with others and experience situations throughout our lives, we inadvertently take on unwanted energies from them. Some of those energies "stick" in the energy fields of our etheric cocoons. When they do, we can begin to experience a variety of difficulties ranging from a lack of focus to physical anomalies in our bodies.

When we act from within our Seventh Sense™, we can see or sense these unwanted energies and remove them. Once removed, the difficulties and physical anomalies disappear and return to states of healthfulness.

These cocoons can also become torn or damaged. This usually occurs in traumatic situations such as events when there is serious physical or emotional trauma.

When this happens, we are less energetically protected and can actually lose energy from within our personal fields or take on way too much energy from others or our environments. These damages may be repaired from within the Seventh Sense™ as well.

Figure 19: Our Etheric Cocoon

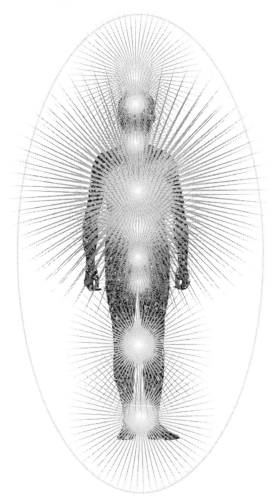

Our etheric cocoon is our transmitter and receiver within the universal construct. We send out energies from within this cocoon which are interpreted by all the particulates with which the energy comes in contact. Conversely, our energetic cocoon translates to us the energies that we receive from the universal communications system.

Our Major Power Centers

Our etheric makeup is comprised of major power centers which include a central highway through which our life energy travels. This highway is most often called our pranic tube.

The pranic tube runs down through the crown of our head and exits near the end of our spine. It is through our crown that incoming, life-sustaining energies enter our fields. From there, the energies move through various avenues throughout our makeup, replenishing old energies with fresh, clear and healthful energies.

As our energy moves through the pranic tube, at certain intervals it supplies our next major energy centers, the chakras. Our chakras are located throughout our bodies, as well as above and below them. There are seven chakra centers which are located within our actual body and five others that are located above and below our bodies (see Figure 20).

Each chakra level has a different frequency and meaning to our functioning. Each chakra demonstrates its frequency by appearing as a specific color. One way to distinguish malfunctioning chakras is by variances in those colors.

Those chakras which are within us are the crown, third eye, throat, heart, solar plexus, second chakra and the root chakra. Usually if there is a dysfunction in one chakra area, there is another chakra that correlates with it. In other words, if there are fragmentations or other malfunctions in the throat chakra area which have led to mistrust or failure to express one's feelings, the second chakra will often show that the client has experienced a very dominating relationship with a parent or other authority figure. The correlations between the chakra areas have countless relationships and combinations.

When I am viewing the chakra areas of my clients, not only do I see the functioning of the energies, but each chakra tells me a story about the experiences of my client. To me, this occurs in the form of little movies with a lot of symbolism intertwined in the story, which means that I must also intuitively interpret what I see. These stories are always accurate and often exhibit the cause for whatever complaint the client has brought.

The chakras often show past life experiences or current or past events that the client has experienced. This is a great tool for understanding the situations facing my clients.

The chakra centers are not merely rotating circular fields of energy as many believe. Rather, they are pyramidal in form with each pyramid having a spiral inside. Each spiral has a normal direction of spin within the pyramid form. If the direction of spin becomes reversed, the chakra center ceases to function normally. Other affectations of note are that the pyramids may become fragmented or actually turn upside down. When the polarities are reversed, the chakra center then becomes abnormal in its functioning and adverse experiences may occur (see Figure 21).

There are many reasons why a chakra may function abnormally. Emotional trauma or physical injury appear to be the most often occuring of these. As human beings, we have a tendency to store the energy of painful emotions within our bodies. As we do so, our energetic systems will reroute themselves or become blocked. Some areas, such as our organs, may become starved for energy and become diseased or cease functioning. Other areas may become overcharged with too much energy which often causes us physical pain.

When we hide the energies of painful feelings from ourselves we run the risk of ultimately becoming sick or experiencing pain within our bodies. In order to normalize our energetic systems we must learn to let go of those old emotions.

Usually those emotions are based upon our interactions with other people which caused us to feel powerless or insignificant. We feel injured and useless, abandoned or betrayed.

What we do not often realize is that those whom we feel have injured us in some way most often have no idea of the impact that they have had on our lives. Or, that their behaviors were generally due to dysfunction brought on by their life experiences!

The damage that we do to ourselves is generally due to our view of separateness from all other things, which we now know is not the case. The separate point of view is one that our egos create in an attempt to help us feel important.

So, let's change that point of view!

Since we are all created of the Light which originated at the Source, and we will ultimately return to that form at some point in our journeys, we know that we are whole and perfect just as we are! We can then begin to see ourselves as beings of value, of innate perfection. In doing so, we realize that there are none greater or lesser than we are – just beings who are at different levels of learning and experience!

When we begin to function from a sense of perfection, releasing feelings and ideas that we are less than perfect, our lives begin to change. We begin to have more positive experiences and those which are not become less and less.

We begin to attract others to our experience who are functioning in a positive manner. Opportunities begin to present themselves to us which we would not have been able to see from a perspective of seeing ourselves as less than perfect!

Figure 20: Pranic Tube and Chakra Positions

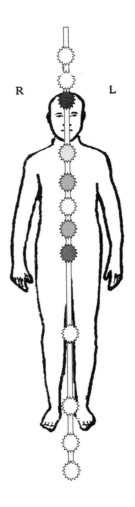

Figure 21: Chakra Pyramid Alignments

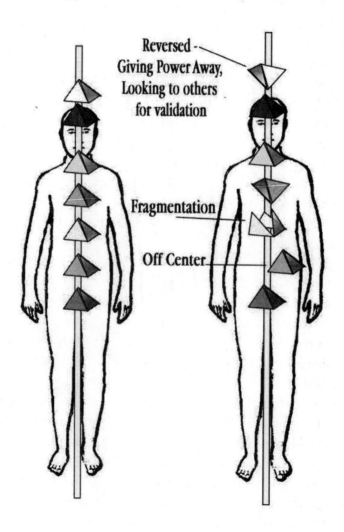

**Normal Pyramid
Alignment**

**Abnormal Pyramid
Alignments**

Reversed -
Giving Power Away,
Looking to others
for validation

Fragmentation

Off Center

Gridlines, Meridians and Axiom Points

In and around our physical bodies are lines of energy that course through all our energetic fields. These are gridlines.

Gridlines are lines of energy that are a part of our makeup and connect us to all other fields of energy within the universal construct. These lines are infinite and continue to move through the universal process, carrying information along the way.

They are a matrix of energy lines that provide us with incoming and outgoing energy much in the way of the pranic tube, except the gridlines look like a giant checker board. The difference is that these lines help us sustain the energy that we receive. These gridlines are our etheric equalizers. In addition, the areas where these lines cross are subtle points within our bodies and etheric fields that, if malfunctioning, can cause physical symptoms.

We can imagine these crosspoints as layers of checker boards through and around us. Occasionally when energy becomes stuck in one of those crosspoints, the energy becomes dense and stagnant or overcharged. This can cause physical illness or pain because that area of the body is no longer receiving the energetic nourishment it needs, or is getting too much energy and that may be painful.

This type of affectation may also occur within our meridian lines. Our meridian lines are major and minor roadways for the energy in our physical bodies. Along our meridian lines are subtle points of energy transfer and exchange. These points may become "switched off" which stops or backs up the energy flow just like a blockage in our plumbing pipes. Clogged meridian points can cause symptoms or illness wherever in the body these points are related. Acupressure and acupuncture were developed centuries ago on this theory.

When working within our Seventh Sense™, we can see and feel the areas that are clogged or overcharged. By touching the affected area and another point at the same time, we instruct the affected point to normalize while maintaining balance within the rest of the body.

Gridlines as well as our meridian lines have major crosspoints within the matrix of the universal grid. Those crosspoints are our axiom points. These points are extremely important to our physical and etheric well being (see Figure 22).

We have several layers of grid lines and axiom points. If we could see the different layered formations of axiom points, we would notice that they form a spiral patterning. This spiral pattern is the same one described by the Fibonacci sequence in Chapter Four. This mathematical sequence also describes consciousness as the sacred spiral and describes the basic format of all creation.

The primary two sets of axiom points are depicted in Figure 22. The inner set of axiom points in this figure crosses at just about the heart chakra area. This set of axiom points includes major meridian points that affect our bodies directly when they become dysfunctional.

There is another major etheric connection that we have at that same point, which is a cord of energy that connects us to the Source, the Light from which we came.

The next most vital area is where the grid lines that run through the outer axiom points in Figure 22 cross just above our second chakra area. These are a fundamental connection to the universal information grid and to our health as well. Again, in this area there is an etheric cord of light which connects us to the Source.

When we have suffered major illness, injury or trauma in our third dimensional existence, those instances can affect the axiom points in our etheric fields. These areas may become damaged. The axiom points may become overcharged with energy or blocked. When this occurs, there can be major adverse affectations in the experience of the client. From within the Seventh Sense™, the axiom points can be repaired to normal functioning.

Figure 22: Axiom Points

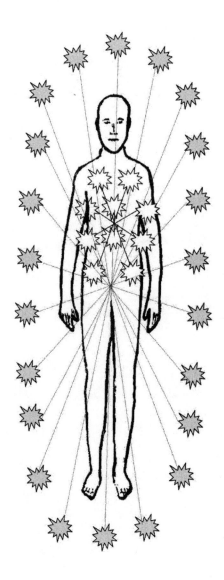

The Etheric Bodies

We exist on more than one level. Part of how we do this is that we have many bodies that contribute to our experience on this plane. Those bodies, our etheric bodies, appear in a specific order, and each of those bodies has a particular function (see Figure 23).

The etheric body that resides closest to our physical body is the emotional body. A healthy emotional body is a magnificent, calm cerulean blue, a silver blue. It is about the same size as the physical body. The emotional body is more highly affected by our experience as human beings than any of our other bodies. It shows the emotional traumas that we have experienced as well as many of our insecurities and emotional injuries. The emotional body is the largest etheric contributor to our physical disorders and pain.

The mental body is just above the emotional body. A clear healthy mental body is a brilliant yellow. When we get stuck in our heads, trying to rationalize or justify our experiences, our mental bodies become inflamed with red energies that usually begin in the head area and move down the center of the mental body. Like the emotional body, when there are abnormalities in the mental body we may experience physical dysfunction.

Next, above our mental body, is our intuitive body. It is from this level that we begin to see beyond our third dimensional experience. The intuitive body is mostly white with a mantle of violet purple over the shoulders and midsection. There are rarely abnormalities of the intuitive body. The most common dysfunction is underuse. When this body is not used often, it becomes undersized and in need of a "recharge".

Figure 23: Order of Etheric Bodies

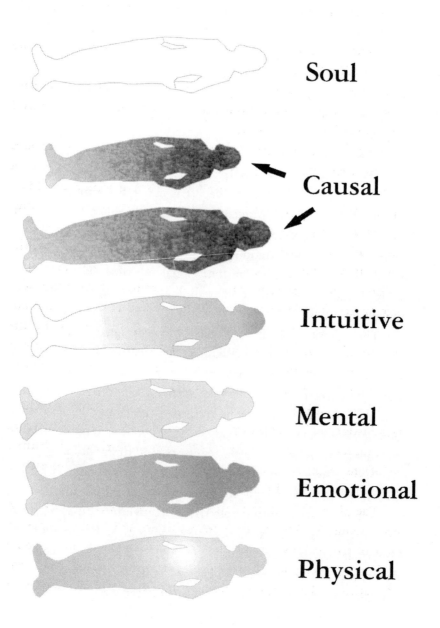

Soul

Causal

Intuitive

Mental

Emotional

Physical

Above the intuitive body reside two ancient aspects of us. These are our causal bodies. The Masters tell me that these bodies are of the "beforetimes", which means before recorded history. These bodies are a magnificent mixture of teals and greens and have much texture to them. The causal bodies often demonstrate the effects of our past lives, those which we experienced before the manifestation of the world as we now know it. These bodies have traveled as early manifestations of us and are our most powerful aspects next to our soul selves.

Our soul bodies are almost always perfect. It is the area around them that becomes affected with various aspects of dysfunction. For instance, a person who has a tendency to hold on to old issues or emotional experiences, who holds their feelings very closely, may demonstrate compressed energy patterns around the soul body. When this occurs, on a third dimensional level the client may experience lack of focus, inability to make quick decisions, or a general lack of direction. They may also demonstrate huge resistance to change. This is because the soul body is not receiving information fully, as it is blocked by the condensed energies. Once these energies are cleared and returned to normal functioning, one can begin to experience clearer understanding of one's direction as well as no resistance to change.

Other affectations around the soul body include demonstrations of karmic situations that are both completed and in progress. Occasionally there are indications of karmic situations that have not yet occurred. The importance of each is generally represented symbolically.

The physical body is remarkable in that it can literally tell a story about the life and experiences of an individual. Different areas of the body, when affected by illness or injury, can give an accurate indication as to the underlying reasons for the affectations. These reasons may include relationship issues with other people, whether they are family or otherwise, hidden emotions and other causes (see Figure 24).

Interestingly, I have found remarkable consistency in demonstration of these causes in the physical body. Figure 24 contains some examples of this. These demonstrations by the body can be quite helpful in counseling the client!

Figure 24: The Body Tells a Story

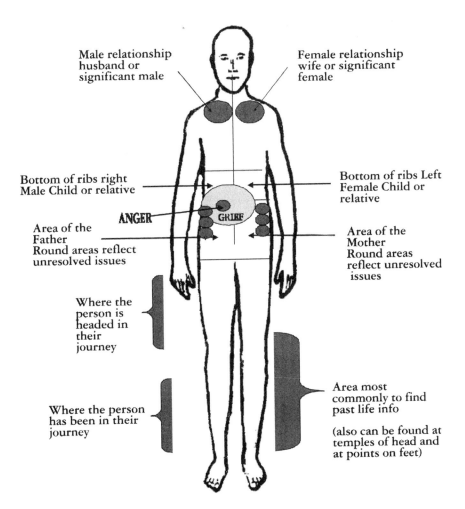

Male relationship husband or significant male

Female relationship wife or significant female

Bottom of ribs right Male Child or relative

Bottom of ribs Left Female Child or relative

ANGER

GRIEF

Area of the Father Round areas reflect unresolved issues

Area of the Mother Round areas reflect unresolved issues

Where the person is headed in their journey

Where the person has been in their journey

Area most commonly to find past life info

(also can be found at temples of head and at points on feet)

This concludes a very basic description of our etheric anatomy. Once we become aware of our many aspects, our etheric bodies, our energy fields, all of the subtle places that we may become affected in our daily lives, it becomes easy to realize that we are not only physical human beings, but rather complex multi-dimensional beings as well.

Further, it becomes quite clear why all causes of illness do not show up on standard medical tests, and why some people remain sick even though their symptoms have been treated by every conceivable cure.

In order to establish complete healthfulness, we must address every aspect on every level. To do this, we must set aside all misconceptions that we are just physical entities and begin to attend to all of the etheric aspects that make us whole. Then and only then will we become perfectly balanced and well.

Full Circle

This brings us to a close for now. The rest is up to you, the reader. Everything that you have read here is true. How you choose to apply what you have learned is entirely up to you. The first thing to remember is not to hold your breath when you think of new possibilities or of changing your reality.

You can do whatever you believe!

So relax, know that change only happens when it is time for us to take a new direction, learn new things, or begin anew. Breaking out of our old standards and models of reality can be a great thing. So what if it means we must venture out of our safety zones? Generally speaking, those safety zones are created by others and are based on fear. Fear of non compliance. Fear of success or failure. Fear of losing someone's love or approval. Fear of what might happen if.... As I said in the Introduction of this book, it takes a lot of courage to step out of that comfort zone. There are many of us out here already and it is an awesome place to be!

In the course of this book, we have traveled through creation, learned about the principles of manifestation, consciousness and how all these things are related. From there, we learned not only how our consciousness works outside our physical realities, but how to access and utilize our consciousness multi-dimensionally by entering the Gamma state. We learned some of the things that being in that state can mean to our creative processes as well as our very existences. From there, we learned a basic anatomy of our etheric selves.

In many ways, these different topics seem to be separate but related parts of a vast body of knowledge. It is more than that. *It is all the same.*

Our very existences are based upon the harmonic relationships of the Light within each of us, our surroundings, our world and the Universe. Everything that we are, all that we do and all that we share in every instance and with other beings is linked eternally.

Knowing this, we can shed any fears that we might have of our mortality as human beings. Without fear of mortality we shed countless other fears as well.

We know that our consciousness is infinite. Our bodies are merely the suits we choose to wear for a time. At some point we will change our cosmic outfits to something else in some other time or place that fits us better. Everything that we have ever done will be remembered within our being. Always.

Every one of our particulates responds to all other happenings throughout the Universe and all its intricacies. The Light within us remembers all that we experience, just as it has since the Beginning.

If we pay attention to our selves on our innermost levels, we can learn to become aware of even the most subtle changes within ourselves, as we develop our Seventh Sense™ and at the same time, a cosmic awareness.

We *are* One with all aspects of creation – with the capabilities to participate within those other realities and to create other realities that we desire. Once we enter the Gamma state, our intentions move through the universal process faster than the speed of light. Energetically we can tell all of creation what we need, want, feel, desire and more. When we do this, we manifest different realities.

When we begin to understand our simple harmonic relationships within the universal construct we come full circle.

We can no longer see ourselves as separate entities that are isolated worlds within themselves but rather as cooperative and co-creative aspects within the living universe.

From there, we become unlimited in our power to create, change, learn, heal, teach and share from the standpoint of those aspects which we are.

The truth is that each of us has an unlimited menu of choices. We can decide to participate – to any degree that we consciously desire – in the creation of greater realities for ourselves, our environments and our world. We can take this knowledge and experience other dimensions, meet and interact with beings of higher vibrational frequencies than ours, visit other times, places or events. Or, we can be content in the knowing that there is so much more out there... What we do and where we choose to go is unlimited, because beyond the third dimension are boundless worlds.

Some may choose to remain within the illusions of the physical world and that is okay. Each of us exists within our own sets of harmonics. We all have lessons to learn, Karmic situations to resolve, experiences that we must have in order to graduate from one frequency of Light to the next. Just as the Light moves through its spectrum of colors, so are we – each as an aspect of that Light – moving through our own spectrum of experiences. Each experience brings us closer to where we began. Closer to the very Source, that which is Light. We must not judge ourselves or others in a comparative nature, but rather see each other as mirrors to our selves in all that we do.

Each of our paths and passages are episodes of color in our spectrum of life. We choose our direction in every moment that we exist. Which road we travel is up to us. And what we do along the way is up to us too.

Only we choose our paths – and there is always a choice.

Will we choose consciously, participating as an intentional aspect of the creation of that which we seek, or will we simply ride along with the tide of concrete reality which is based not upon the laws of the Universe, but upon physical and tangible perceptions set forth by those who came before us? Will we continue to follow those who instill within us their ignorance of anything beyond third dimensional reality and all things beyond simple logic? I hope not.

When we choose consciously, our value systems change. We no longer see things the way we did. What we thought was really important in our day-to-day lives changes dramatically. The "drama and trauma", as the Masters call it, is no longer effective to us. We begin to function from states of higher awareness and, from there, become more and more in tune with all other aspects of creation. This affects how we live, how we relate with others, and what we share of ourselves as well as what we receive.

Our lives become heart centered. We begin to see the intricacies within all relationships. We become capable of instantly manifesting *whatever* we intend because we are working as an integral part of the One. In essence, we are all that we have ever sought. Right here. Right now. We are the power.

For it is that when we recognize ourselves as the Light, the Supreme Being, the Creator of our realities, we discover that everything we have searched for is within our very selves.

We become fluid in the creation of our reality, our destiny, our lifetimes and all the experiences that we have within them. No longer are there boxes around our experiences. The old rules don't apply. We no longer have to "go with the flow"; we *are* the flow.

The Masters have always told me that

"*...when the pure of heart meets with the pureness of being in all its innocence is born a harmony with all things...*"

Simply, we *become*. And the possibilities are unlimited.

About the Author

Dr. Meg Blackburn Losey is an internationally recognized Author, Master Healer, Channeler, speaker and graphic artist. Her Channelings are distributed to subscribers globally as the "Online Channelings and Messages".

She is an Ordained Minister in both Spiritual Science and Metaphysics. Meg has a Ph.D. in Holistic Life Counseling and a Doctoral Degree in Metaphysics. She is a medical intuitive and a certified practitioner of Spiritual Mind Healing. Meg is the developer of Seventh Sense™ Attunement and Movement to Spirit™. She resides in the mountains of Tennessee.

Please visit Meg's website at http://www.spiritlite.com for her current newsletters and her appearance and workshop schedule. Meg may be reached via e-mail at meg@spiritlite.com.

The Spirit Light Teaching Series

For further information or bookings, please contact Meg at:

Spirit Light Resources
P.O. Box 625
Andersonville, TN 37705

Or by e-mail at
meg@spiritlite.com

LIVE GROUP CHANNELING • Dr. Meg Blackburn Losey brings the Ascended Masters to you live and in person, with messages of the moment or specific subjects, and allowing an open forum to answer your questions. This is a powerful experience as the Masters convey energetic attunements throughout their presence with you. Warm, loving and humorous, the Ascended Masters always amaze group participants with their understanding and compassion and ability to speak about an unlimited range of subjects.

MOVEMENT TO SPIRIT™ • The ever popular interactive workshop which teaches the participant how to utilize energy, music and movement toward opening to Gamma Consciousness, our highest consciousness. Includes an explanation of the basic Universal principles and how the consciousness may be used for manifestation, healing, learning and participating in holographic reality. If your attempts to meditate have met with little or no success, this workshop gives you a fun and easy alternative that works!

PYRAMIDS OF LIGHT, Awakening to Multi-Dimensional Realities™ • How do we manifest the reality that we desire? How do miracles happen? Can we really produce them? Is this reality an illusion? What is the connection between our consciousness and our body? Are we *really* part of everything? What is "the Light"? Can we travel in time to other places, events, even our future? Learn the answers to these questions and more as Dr. Blackburn weaves a straightforward yet comprehensive account of the universal construct, its relationship with sacred geometry, the manifestation of matter, consciousness, and the harmonic relationship of all things beyond quantum physics and the fabric of all creation to this here and now. This workshop is your attunement to the Seventh Sense™, your highest state of perception! Explore the science of consciousness and its relationship within the universal construct. Learn how to become multi-dimensionally aware and how to apply these techniques to create unlimited possibilities within your life and the lives of others. Use your consciousness *within* the Universal construct acting as a part of the One. You are the creator that you seek! This seminar includes the popular Movement to Spirit™ as a tool for gaining higher consciousness awareness!

HEALING THROUGH THE SEVENTH SENSE™ • *Taught in conjunction with Pyramids of Light workshop as a two or three day intensive workshop. "Pyramids of Light" is a prerequisite to this course.* Learn how to apply your Seventh Sense™ toward healing yourself and others while working interactively within the holographic realms. Learn to intensify and focus energies, use other-dimensional tools, work with the etheric bodies, and change the particulate arrangement, the very essence of creation, toward healthfulness and wholeness. Learn how to read the body to discover issues in this and past lives, to adjust the different energy centers, grid points, axiom points, and to align, balance and manifest healing. Begin to read the relationships between the energy fields...the body truly does tell a story! Understand how to affect aspects that are far out into the dimensional realms to address concurrent existences. Includes practice sessions. (*This is an advanced course in sensitivity beyond the local reality. It is inter-dimensionally oriented and energy intensive. Recommended for advanced students of Metaphysics.*)

Bibliography

Aivanhov, Omraam Mikhael, "**The Symbolic Language of Geometrical Figures**", Prosveta S.A., Frejus, France, 1990.

Ayrmetes Corporation web site, Advanced Cognitive Technologies "Decoding Brain Waves", http://ayrmetes.com/articles/decoding_brain_waves.htm, October 2003.

Brennan, Barbara Ann, "**Hands of Light**, A Guide to Healing Through the Human Energy Field", Bantam Books, June 1988.

Cambridge Relativity: Quantum Gravity: "**M-theory formerly known as Strings**", http://www.damtp.cam.uk/user/gr/public/qg_ss.html, March, 2003.

Curcio, Kimberly Panisset, "**Man of Light**", Select Books Inc., NY, NY, 2002.

Davies, Paul, New York Times, "**A Brief History of the Multiverse**", http://www.nytimes.com/2003/04/12/opinion/12DAVI.html?pag ewanted=1&th, April 12, 2003.

Gardner, Laurence, "**Bloodline of the Holy Grail**", Fair Winds Trade Press, Gloucester, MA, 2002.

Gardner, Lawrence, "**Lost Secrets of the Sacred Ark**", Element (Harper Collins) Hammersmith, London, 2003.

Glanz, James, NYTimes.com, Archive, Late Edition-Final, section A, Page 12, Column 1, "**Studies Suggest Unknown Form of Matter Exists**", http://query.nytimes.com/gst/abstract.html?res=F50D15FD355C OC728FDDAE0894DA40..., July 31, 2002.

Gowan, John A., "Principles of a Unified Field theory: A Tetrahedral Model, Cornell University Web Site, http://www.people.cornell.edu/pages/jag8/trintxt.html, March 29, 2002.

Gowan, John, "Symmetry Principles of the Unified Field Theory" Cornell University Web Site, http://www.people.cornell.edu/pages/jag8index.html, November 27, 2000.

Gray, Henry, "Gray's Anatomy", fifteenth edition, Barnes and Nobles Books, 1995.

http://www.brainmachines.com/frequencies.htm, "Brain Wave Frequencies", October 2003.

http://www.geocities.com, "Introduction on the Golden Ratio and Fibonacci Numbers", http://www.geocities.com/jyce3/intor.com, June, 2003.

Jefferys, Prof. John, "Brain Waves ("40 Hz") Research" University of Birmingham Neurophysiology Department , University of Birmingham website, http://medweb.bham.ac.uk/neuroscience/jefferys/jjwaves.htm, October 2003.

Lokhorst, Gert-Jan C. "The Originality of Descartes' Theory About the Pineal Gland", *Journal for the History of Neuro Sciences,* 10 (1):6-18, 2001. ISSN 0964-704X.

Melchizedek, Drunvalo, "The Ancient Flower of Life", Volume 1, Light Technology Publishing, Flagstaff, AZ, 1998.

Melchizedek, Drunvalo, "The Ancient Flower of Life", Volume 2, Light Technology Publishing, Flagstaff, AZ, 2000.

Miller, Iona and Miller, Richard Allen, "**From Helix to Hologram, An Ode on the Human Genome**", Nexus Magazine, September-October, 2003, Volume 10, No.5, Page 47.

Neuro Therapy Center for Health, "**Neuro Therapy, The Heart and Science of Healing**", http://www.winfd.com/bra.htm , October, 2003.

NYTimes.com, Archive, Late Edition, section A, Page 13, Column 1, "**Einstein Was Right on Gravity's Velocity**", http://query.nytimes.com/gst/abstract.html?res=FAOA1FFC385 AOC7B8CDDA80894DB4...January 8, 2003.

Pond, Dale, "**Universal Laws Never Before Revealed: Keely's Secrets**", The Message Company, Santa Fe, NM, 2000.

Talbot, Michael, "**The Holographic Universe**", Harper Collins, NY, NY, 1992.

Vasant Corporation, "**About Spin Waves**", http://www.vasantcorporation.com/about_spin_waves.html, March, 2003.

Wilson, Colin, "**From Atlantis to the Sphinx**", Fromm International Publishing Co., NY, NY, 1997.

Spirit Light Resources Catalog

(More items available at http://www.spiritlite.com)

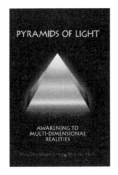

"Pyramids of Light"

A fantastic journey from the beginning of creation, manifestation of realities, and on through the science of consciousness and how to work within the universal construct to intentionally manifest whatever reality you desire! A must read!

_____ Copies @ $18.95 $_____

Movement to Spirit™ Live Workshop CD
A great companion CD to the book "Pyramids of Light". This workshop takes the participant into Gamma Consciousness through fun, easy-to-do movement with music!

_____ CD's @ $19.95 $_____

The following are read-only CDs (not sound) intended for use on your computer. They require Adobe Acrobat to open. This program may be obtained free at adobe.com:

The Online Channelings and Messages 2002
The complete unedited collection of Meg's Online Channelings and Messages, 2002. Bonus feature included on this CD is Meg's channeled art work "The Traveler"!

_____ CD's @ $19.95 $_____

S&H is $4.95 for the first item and $1.00 for each item thereafter.
Please send to Spirit Light Resources, POB 625, Andersonville, TN 37705

The Arcturian Corridor Series

The complete unedited set of Channelings and excerpts from Channelings that explains in detail what the multi-dimensional opening of the Arcturian Corridor means to us now and in the future!

_____ CD's @ $19.95 $_____

Meg Blackburn Losey's Channeled Artwork
(more selections may be found at http://www.spiritlite.com)

"Enlightened Journey" A reminder to us all that once we release our spirits we can soar with boundless freedom!

A full color print on high gloss Kodak photo paper. Suitable for framing to enhance any room!

_____ 8 ½ x 11 Prints @ $15.95 $_____

"Octave" The expression of a musical octave geometrically as a reminder that all things are in harmonic balance from the smallest to the largest scale of Being.

A full color print on high gloss Kodak photo paper. Suitable for framing to enhance any room!

_____ 8 ½ x 11 Prints @ $15.95 $_____

S&H is $4.95 for first item and $1.00 for each item thereafter.
Please send to Spirit Light Resources, POB 625, Andersonville, TN 37705

"Balance" When we are of perfect harmony within ourselves, our environment, our worlds, we become of balance in all ways, being an integral part of the natural flow of life and being...

A full color print on high gloss Kodak photo paper. Suitable for framing to enhance any room!

_____ 8 ½ x 11 Prints @ $15.95 $_____

"Regeneration" Reminds us all to take the time to regenerate spiritually, mentally, emotionally and spiritually, and that we have far more to draw from than we often remember.

A full color print on high gloss Kodak photo paper. Suitable for framing to enhance any room!

_____ 8 ½ x 11 Prints @ $15.95 $_____

"One Light" is what we become when we give ourselves in love not from need, but as one whole who, with another, becomes an enhanced One...

A full color print on high gloss Kodak photo paper. Suitable for framing to enhance any room!

_____ 8 ½ x 11 Prints @ $15.95 $_____

S&H is $4.95 for first item and $1.00 for each item thereafter.
Please send to Spirit Light Resources, POB 625, Andersonville, TN 37705

"Tandem Flight" Lovers are mirrors to each other in every way. This reflection can be done freely, creating lightness within the relationship.

A full color print on high gloss Kodak photo paper. Suitable for framing to enhance any room!

_____ 8 ½ x 11 Prints @ $15.95 $_____

"The Traveler" Reminds us that we are not alone in the universe, that multi-dimensional travel is not only possible but a common occurrence.

A full color print on high gloss Kodak photo paper. Suitable for framing to enhance any room!

_____ 8 ½ x 11 Prints @ $15.95 $_____

"Fairie Nights" A reminder to us all to find the child within, our innocent selves that were buried long ago. When we touch our innocence we remember how to fly!

A full color print on high gloss Kodak photo paper. Suitable for framing to enhance any room!

_____ 8 ½ x 11 Prints @ $15.95 $_____

S&H is $4.95 for first item and $1.00 for each item thereafter.
Please send to Spirit Light Resources, POB 625, Andersonville, TN 37705

Order Form

Books & CD's

Pyramids of Light _____ Copies @ $18.95 $_____

Movement to Spirit™ Workshop CD
_____ CD's @ $19.95 $_____

Online Channeling and Messages 2002 CD
_____ CD's @ $19.95 $_____

The Arcturian Corridor Series _____ CD's @ $19.95 $_____

Artwork

Enlightened Journey _____ 8 ½ x 11 Prints @ $15.95 $_____

Octave _____ 8 ½ x 11 Prints @ $15.95 $_____

Balance _____ 8 ½ x 11 Prints @ $15.95 $_____

Regeneration _____ 8 ½ x 11 Prints @ $15.95 $_____

One Light _____ 8 ½ x 11 Prints @ $15.95 $_____

Tandem Flight _____ 8 ½ x 11 Prints @ $15.95 $_____

Subtotal: $_____

Shipping & Handling: (All items sent first class US Mail unless otherwise arranged.) Please add $4.95 for the first item and $1.00 for each item thereafter. (International orders except Canada, please add an additional $5.00 for the first item and $2.00 for each additional item.)

$$\text{S\&H} \quad \$\underline{\hspace{2cm}}$$

$$\text{TOTAL ENCLOSED} \quad \$\underline{\hspace{2cm}}$$

Thank you!

Shipping Information

Name: _____

Telephone: _____

Shipping
Address: _____

City, State,
ZIP: _____

Country: _____

Please send this form with a check or money order to:

**Spirit Light Resources, P.O. Box 625, Andersonville, TN 37705
Attention: Book Orders**

VISIT http://www.spiritlite.com FOR OUR FULL CATALOG!